Complete
Memories of a Climb

Michael French

Print ISBN: 979-8-9874087-0-4

A mas no poder...

Contents

Preface

This is a personal account of the first alpine-style ascent of the Messner Route on the South Face of Aconcagua (22,838 feet), Argentina, the highest mountain in the Southern and Western hemispheres.

It should be noted that our initial several pitches were to the left of the line of the first ascent by the French expedition of 1954. That line is classic and is known as "The French Route." It begins on the right side of the foot of the central pillar and goes up the extreme left-hand side of the big couloir for a ways, then follows a steep ramp up to the top of the promontory itself.

We, however, began our climb on the left-hand side of the great promontory and buttress that lies at the foot of the central rib and worked our way up to the top of the promontory and the central pillar where the French Route comes in from the right. This variation is known today as the Slovene or Slovenian variant to the French Route. It was named after an ascent by a group of outstanding Slovenian climbers on January 22, 1982 – Milan Crnilogar, Igor Skamperle, Slavko Sveticic and Bogdan Biscak.

Brian Berg, Hugh Grandfield and I climbed that variant in March of 1980, continued on the French Route and then onto the Messner exit or finish. Brian and I summited on March 14, 1980.

While I write this in the present day (2021-2022), the events related here all took place in the past. Although memory is subject to change, I have used personal notes, cassette recordings, short written letters and diary entries, newspaper accounts, published and unpublished articles and calendars to reconstruct a narrative as accurately as I can. It is a recount of the climb and how I arrived at the point where I accepted Brian's invitation to join his endeavor. It is a narrative of struggle, tragedy, survival and success.

Any person mentioned here, by name or nickname, is real – and if there are any misspellings, they are mine, and not intentional. The events, situations and circumstances are also real and occurred. While I describe them as accurately as I can, undoubtedly there would be slightly different retellings by different people. If anything, a reader may find a tendency toward understatement, a little sarcasm and stoicism. Indeed, these traits are a part of my personality. I do not lightly or readily share my emotions or thoughts, and this account, long overdue, has helped bring closure.

I held most talented climbers of the day (late '70s), both well-known and relatively unknown, in high regard, hoping to climb at some small measure of their expertise. The great alpinists of the day pushed the mountaineering envelope in such a way that alpinism and climbing were forever changed. The alpine-style ascent of Everest without oxygen in 1978 by Rheinhold Messner and Peter Habeler was, in my opinion, one of the defining moments in climbing big mountains. I am in absolute awe of today's breed of alpinists. I'm not sure if they are from the same planet as I am. They are truly wizards.

Hugh, Brian and I were not professional climbers. We

were amateurs. Brian and I had jobs that required intense effort, dedication and time. Besides climbing, our other duties involved high-risk activities and we were responsible for those working for us, so climbing, while a passion, was not 'what we did.' We all three were passionate about mountaineering and climbing and did so whenever we could. We were decent climbers for sure, though we didn't consider ourselves particularly gifted, nor extraordinarily talented. We were, however, bold, stubborn and persistent. Persistent, some would say, to an extreme.

Dedication

This account is dedicated to the memory of Hugh Grandfield, who saved my life during the ascent, but who did not live to see the summit.

Acknowledgements

This narrative also commemorates the memory of Brian Berg, a friend, a comrade in arms and a fellow United States Air Force PJ (Pararescueman). It was Brian who put the three of us together, who led our group, and whose prompting propelled us to this world-class climb. Brian would later die (1994) pretty much in my arms at 14,000 feet on the side of a volcano in Mexico, following a violent canopy collapse and severe crash while paragliding. We had gone there to train for what was to be another extreme endeavor.

In this account, I use excerpts – quoted verbatim – directly from Brian's journal to both highlight and to counterpoint my own memory and recounting.

In particularly difficult moments during the descent and trek back towards civilization with thawed frozen toes, feet and fingers, I found strength and resolve in thinking of my fellow pararescuemen. These were, and are, friends and brothers, at my home unit and elsewhere, whom I could not, would not – and did not – let down by giving up. Whether you knew it or not, you were part and parcel of my return.

In the intervening years since this climb, I have been lucky to find people who wanted to hear about it. For those who were willing to actually listen, I recounted most parts of it. Almost everyone told me, "you should write a book."

Then one day not too long ago, I was in the Caribbean in St. Lucia sitting on a catamaran that some friends and I had bareboat chartered, and after a beer or two and some prompting, I repeated much of the story. Again, I heard: "you should write a book." But this time, it was from a friend, Robert (Bob) Lamont, who I figured should really know, as he is an author. His encouragement moved me off dead center and was what I needed to get started.

In cross-checking my own recollection about our climb and researching more recent information about additional routes and changes, I came across a climbing guidebook by R.J. Secor called *Aconcagua: A Climbing Guide* (second edition), published by The Mountaineers. I found it to be superb.

Josiah and Karesse Duhaime, friends at the marina from which I now sail, asked me one day if I would share my recollection of the climb with them. I did. That led to more detailed retellings of many specific parts of the climb and through their questions, surfaced memories I did not think were still present. While sitting on their beautiful sailboat one evening, and after sharing the many trials, near deaths, the loss of Hugh and suffering severe frostbite, Karesse asked me **how** I felt upon finally reaching the summit. In all the years since the climb, I don't remember anyone asking that direct question before, and I had never formulated an answer. Without any hesitation or thought, I responded, "complete."

Most recently, on a sailing trip to Ensenada, Mexico, I mentioned to friends, Drew Hare and Leah Arruda, that I was nearing the end of the first draft of this account, and Leah volunteered to help with editing. I could not believe my good fortune. In addition to editing, she has become a guiding light and mentor. Without her input I would still be stumbling around trying to figure out what needed addressing and what needed deleting.

Complete
Memories of a Climb

1

Beginnings

Portland, Oregon
304th Aerospace Rescue and Recovery Squadron
U.S. Air Force Reserve (USAFR)

I could hear the APU (auxiliary power unit) crank up right outside my office window and knew that the maintenance guys were about to do an engine run up on one of our helicopters. Soon, the tips of its rotor blades would be spinning some 20 feet from my desk, making everything inside this part of the PJ building dance. Thought and conversation on my side of the building would be difficult at best. Time to wander next door to Operations and chat.

Just about then the phone rang, and in 1979, you did the very best you could to actually answer the phone. There was no call back feature, no caller ID, no way to know who was wanting a piece of your time. It turned out to be Brian Berg, a friend and fellow PJ, and by all accounts a bit of a wild character, but then most of us were sort of wild by normal standards. I had to tell him I would call him back as I could barely hear what he was saying. All I could make out was "crazy project" and "stupendous."

By now though, the Huey's engine had spun up to 100% and the engine noise, combined with the rotor noise, were the only things one could hear. Hoping he could hear me, I repeated that I'd call him back and hung up.

Air Force Rescue was, and is, an interesting subset within the USAF and U.S. military. Primarily dedicated to combat search and rescue, units are often tasked with special missions, and on a not-to-interfere basis, may also do civilian SAR (Search and Rescue). And we do civilian SAR very well.

Within this subset are some of the best people in the Air Force, be they admin and maintenance or pilots and crew. Those personnel who have actual hands-on contact with people rescued or things recovered are known as Pararescuemen, or PJs – the most highly-trained and extremely versatile recovery specialists in the world.

I could go on for quite a while as to what a PJ is (or at least what I think a PJ is). It's probably better if you're really interested in knowing, to do the Google search thing for the term *USAF Pararescue*.

Like all our close brothers within the military community,

we are trained in SERE (survival, evasion, resistance, escape) techniques, static-line and free-fall parachuting and jumping with ridiculous equipment, open- and closed-circuit scuba, free-fall swimmer deployment from helicopters, rappelling and fast-roping, climbing, snow and ice travel, small arms use, the occasional aerial gunnery qualification, and the list goes on. However, since our primary mission is rescue, unlike many of our brothers, we are also medics or Emergency Medical Technicians.

Today, operational PJs maintain a higher level of medical qualification than we did...but back in the day we did help set the standard.

To give you an idea of the current level of medical expertise, you should check out an article in the December 26, 2019, issue of Esquire Magazine, titled *Pararescue - The Special Ops Unit That Rescues Navy SEALs*. (And no, the article is not about rescuing Navy SEALs, but rather about a jump mission to a freighter on the high seas that had suffered an explosion and fire involving four seamen, two of whom died and two who were burned critically.)

The ability to use any of the techniques employed by standard or elite U.S. military forces, and being a medic/rescue/recovery specialist, paves the way for small groups of PJs to be deployed and sometimes embedded with other U.S. military units, both in combat and peacetime SAR.

My training days were pretty heady and exhilarating. Can you imagine yourself as a young, 20-something and being paid to learn to scuba dive, skydive, hike, climb, medically treat and rescue people?

A PJ has sometimes been described as a "jack of all trades, master of none." A more correct version might be "jack of all trades, master of some." Due to the geographical location of a unit and the local topography, you would often find PJs gravitating toward a specific skill because it was in their backyard, and they liked it.

A unit in the desert was pretty good at desert operations, a unit on the coast conducted lots of "training" scuba operations/dives. A unit in Alaska was one of the premier units for wilderness rescue. And so on.

My unit at the time of Brian's phone call was the 304th ARRSq, located on Portland Air National Guard Base at the Portland, Oregon International Airport. It was one of six Reserve and Guard USAF rescue units. All six units maintained the same level of currency and qualifications as active duty units. This enabled any one unit, or a current and qualified individual, to be immediately deployed and augment or assume the mission of another squadron.

Sometime later, when the engine and rotor noise stopped, temporarily anyway, I returned Brian's call. He was the

NCOIC (non-commissioned officer in charge) of a small Pararescue Section in a Rescue Detachment at Holloman Air Force Base (AFB), New Mexico. Though never having directly worked together, we had met several times over the course of our careers and based on the limited contact, rumors, tall tales, wild stories and hallway reputation, we respected each other as PJs and as climbers. He was tall, lean, sinewy and had a great strength to weight ratio – pretty much what you wanted in climbing. He had good reach being tall, could hang on to small holds by his fingertips and had developed decent strength in his legs for carrying loads. Somewhat acerbic by nature, you either liked him right off because you were on the same wavelength, or you didn't like him at all. I liked him.

Brian had been stationed in England for several years before being assigned to Holloman, and while there, one of his pastimes was to venture into the British hills, scramble, boulder and climb. While in England he had also managed to get to the Continent and had climbed on the Matterhorn on its classic Hörnli Ridge. All this was as a part time alpinist – the hours you put in as a PJ (or for anyone in the military) can be quite long.

Brian began our conversation by recounting a string of improbable (but mostly true) events on various TDYs (temporary duty assignment away from a home station) we had been on, and then started complimenting me about performance on a climb on Denali I had participated in the year before. I knew at that moment I was being set up for the actual pitch of the conversation. He went on to talk about wanting to scale a peak in South America with a small group of climbers. It wasn't just a peak – it was the highest peak actually – and he wanted to do this on a previously unclimbed route, on the most difficult side of the mountain, alpine style. And, oh, by the way, he was hoping I'd join him.

I couldn't even pronounce the name of the peak much less tell you exactly where it was. To my astonishment, instead of turning him down flat, I said, "maybe...well, probably yes."

A segue about my participation in the earlier climb of Denali.

I had transferred to the 304th ARRSq in Portland from the 303rd ARRSq at March AFB, California (near Riverside). While at March, as an "FNG" (fucking new guy) and rookie, I discovered that I found climbing, and just about everything with it, to be enjoyable. I learned that I loved the smell of the sun warming exposed granite and the feel of an ice axe or ice hammer taking a bite into perfect ice. The exposure to 10, 100 or 1000 vertical feet of air below you was exhilarating, electrifying and terrifying, often all in the same pitch. I discovered that I liked the focus required on moves difficult for me.

That's the same focus that climbers of today so eloquently express as centering, visualization and clearing the mind. I enjoyed the preparation for a climbing trip as well. I was somewhat anal regarding organization. To maximize the time available for actually climbing, I would plan and organize an outing in detail, trying to minimize any loss of time during travel and the approach. I relished poring over older texts on how mountaineering expeditions had been organized and planned.

While I was with the 303rd, the squadron deployed to Alaska several times, both for training and to assist and pull alert for the active duty USAF Rescue unit based outside of Anchorage. There, I renewed friendships with assigned PJs, and was introduced to glacier travel and snow and ice climbing.

Returning to Southern California, I continued to climb when I could, mostly on technical rock, and of course did conditioning runs on and between peaks in SoCal.

Wanting to experience a bit more altitude than what I could find locally in SoCal, I convinced a PJ buddy, Richard (Dick) Grady, to go to Mexico with me and climb the three classic volcanoes: Iztaccihuatl, Popocatépetl, and Pico de Orizaba. None are difficult to climb unless you seek out the most difficult variations of routes simply to do so. They do, however, represent a physiological challenge and will give an aspiring big mountain climber an idea of whether they can actually handle being at or above 18,000 feet.

Dick and I arrived in Mexico City one early afternoon in December 1977, rented a little VW bug and immediately began our drive to the first volcano. After nightfall, we were nearing the Paso de Cortez between Iztaccihuatl and Popocatépetl. Arriving at the Paso de Cortez somewhere around 11 p.m., we parked off the road in a wide pull-out area of some kind and we slept (sort of) in our VW beetle that night.

Getting up early and grumpy but with decent weather, we easily summited Iztaccihuatl (17,160 feet) and returned to the car. After driving in the daylight for only a few minutes, we found a hostel nearby and had a much better second night. The next day we summited Popocatépetl (17,802 feet), and once back at the hostel asked around about how to get to the base of Orizaba (18,491 feet). Based on the conversation flow and map reading, we figured out it was going to take us at least one entire day to re-stage for that attempt.

We blasted out of Paso de Cortez early the next morning and managed to find Tlachichuca, the town from which most climbers staged at the base of Orizaba, by late afternoon. Asking anyone we saw with a sturdy looking vehicle about hiring a 4x4 to transport us and our rucksacks to the trailhead the following day, we eventually found someone who agreed to take us. And as soon as he suggested we could stay at his place overnight to simplify logistics, we agreed.

Turned out he was one of several people with 4x4s who routinely took aspiring climbers to the base of Orizaba. He explained that he had visiting family in the rooms he would normally rent, but that we could stay on the rooftop of his garage if that was okay. It was. His wife had prepared a simple, but very tasty and filling dinner which we devoured. After supper, we spread our sleeping bags and pads underneath the stars and quickly drifted off to sleep.

We were awakened a rather indecently short time later by a series of loud hisses, cracks, booms and bangs, then witnessed the town's fireworks display close on as we were basically directly underneath it. It was the New Year. Back to sleep by 1 a.m.

At around 3 a.m., we awoke again and loaded everything into our new-found friend's Jeep then bounced and lurched to the trail head. Checking out the climbers' hut at the base, we quickly decided we needed to depart ASAP. We did not want to be in the middle of a conga line weaving up the route. We shouldered our rucks, bypassed all the huts you normally stop at, and went directly to the summit. The way down was one long slog. We managed to coordinate for a pickup once at the bottom and were soon back at our car. On to Mexico City – and we actually had a couple of days to tour like a tourist. All in all, not hard, but it did give me a taste for being at 18,000 feet.

About the same time, something known as the USAF High Altitude Rescue Team (HART) was conceived, and its formation approved. In as much as I had now climbed to 18,000 feet, I ended up being nominated to the team and was accepted by the team leaders. Even better, I was to participate in a USAF attempt to summit Denali as a proof of concept. (Imagine...an all-expenses paid trip to Alaska to climb!)

The purpose of the HART was to have a dedicated team of military specialists who could be rapidly deployed anywhere on earth and who could recover items of national interest at high elevations in mountainous terrain. (This was 1978 – there were no helicopters that could fly much above 18,000 feet with a load, hover, land, and take off). While an Air Force High Altitude Rescue Team may seem a bit far-fetched, it actually pales in comparison to other U.S. government (USG) escapades. Once the USG decides it wants to do something, cost and finding expertise are no real objects, and the HART was tame compared to other projects.

A few examples of some truly special endeavors undertaken by the USG include:

- Clandestinely retrieving sunken Soviet submarines from a great depth (*1974, Project Azorian: Soviet Submarine K-129 and the Glomar Explorer*).

- Climbing a 25,000-foot mountain in India and placing a man-portable, nuclear powered, electronic listening post in order to spy on the Chinese (1965-1966, CIA, Operation Hat, Nanda Devi).

- And, in a USAF mission, the mid-air retrieval of de-orbited objects from satellites. In the days before the Space Shuttle and long before digital cameras, film was the medium used by cameras in space. The only way to get the images taken by the cameras was to have the film in a protective cassette or package, jettison it from a satellite and de-orbit it. After re-entry, the package deployed a parachute under which it descended. One of our rescue units had specially equipped aircraft that would fly an intercept and snag the vertical line between the object and its parachute as it was descending. After securing the line, the package swung under and behind the aircraft. Once stabilized, it was reeled inside the back of the aircraft.

  In the very rare case the mid-air retrieval missed, PJs would parachute into the ocean to secure the package and await recovery. Turns out, one of my good buddies and a former roommate, Jack Ergish, was on one of the few such jump missions. (*For more info on the unit and the program, you can online search: USAF To Catch a Falling Star.*)

The development of the HART is superbly addressed in detail in an online article titled "The Air Force's First High Altitude Rescue Team (HART)" by friend and fellow PJ, MSgt John F. Cassidy (*afspecialwarfare.com*).

So it ended up being my "job" to be sent to Alaska, to be with buddies, and to climb Denali...after all these years, I still can't believe that.

Denali beckoned, and I deployed to Alaska to join friends and brothers for the expedition. Under the very capable leadership of Robert (Bob) LaPointe, in May and June of 1978 we put five of ten climbers on the summit via the West Buttress Route. In doing so we demonstrated the ability of a team of Air Force members to deploy, self-sustain for three weeks or more and operate above 18,000 feet. The USAF HART had become reality.

Brian's harebrained scheme was for a team of three – Brian, Hugh Grandfield, who was a younger climbing friend of his from England, and I – to climb an unknown route on the South Face of Aconcagua. The South Face is over 9,000 vertical feet high and has been described as one of the great walls of the world. Looking at the face, the route Brian was proposing was to partially follow a couloir to the left of the line of the original French ascent of 1954, climb up to about 19,000 feet and then traverse right and over onto the exit line done by Reinhold Messner in 1974. Messner's line of ascent followed the French Route from the bottom of the face up to where it veers off to the right on the upper glacier. Messner's variation is more direct and continues slightly left and straight up from that point. From the summit we would descend via the normal route (non-technical) on the north side of the mountain.

The only lines on the Face in 1980: French Route (blue) and Messner variant (red).

As a side note, Brian's proposed route would have been, I believe, the same line that was climbed in an extreme solo ascent in December 2009 by U.S. climber Chad Kellog (the line now known as Medicine Buddha).

As of our planning phase in mid-1979, and some five years after Messner summited via the central pillar direct, he was still the only person to have completed that particular line. All other successful teams who had ascended the South Face had done so by the French Route. And there had only been six or seven successful expeditions to summit via the South Face since 1954. And no one had climbed the South Face alpine style.

You think, *well, really, how difficult can the mountain be?* Today, people climb it all the time, and it has been described as a relatively easy peak with no real technical climbing required. One needs to keep in mind that the world is full of mountains and remote areas that have easy access or lines of ascent on one side, and extreme routes on the other. Aconcagua is one such mountain. The scale of the South Face is astonishing. It is 9,000 feet of near vertical wall. There are hanging glaciers, vertical ice falls and seracs, a few easy rock pitches along with many difficult and complex vertical rock sections hundreds of feet high. There is all manner of challenges. Just to gain the foot of the only route accomplished on the face at the time required one to climb over 2,000 vertical feet of very steep snow, ice and rock. Many sections of the face are continually swept by avalanche and rockfall.

Fun!

Having said to Brian "...maybe, well, probably yes," I still had a small out, or an option to bail. Before I could say no, however, pride now dictated that I needed to at least research Brian's proposed route and indeed, read about the mountain itself.

Easy-peasy, you say...

Hmmm, in 1979, there was no readily available database of routes and climbs. Research for an effort such as we were contemplating was a bit more laborious than one may find today. My bible for researching the South Face became a climbing book, Big Walls by Reinhold Messner, who was without doubt the world's most pre-eminent big-mountain alpinist of that time. I also found some good photos of the South Face (long distance, but excellent quality) in a copy of *National Geographic*.

A study of the photos in those two publications and of loose articles about the first ascent of the South Face by the French in 1954 convinced me that the avalanche danger on the route Brian was proposing was extreme. In fact, I thought it was so extreme that I would not agree to attempt that line. I proposed instead that we follow Messner's route. I added that it would still be an alpine style ascent of the South Face, something that had not yet been accomplished. That Messner could have climbed the South Face alpine style is beyond doubt... it was just that he was with a group of other climbers doing an expedition and they didn't.

Brian didn't agree easily, but he eventually did.

Why the appeal of climbing alpine style vs. expedition style?

There are several reasons really. Among them are tangible ones like the greater financial, logistical and organizational complexities of an expedition. An expedition is very much a team effort, and less of an individual effort. Indeed, for any older expeditions in the Himalayas, often less than half of the climbers were identified for the summit push. By the mid-1970s the organization of an expedition had become sophisticated to the extent that a successful climb was no longer a singular, personal achievement, but rather a testament to the expedition's management and logistical prowess. In an alpine style attempt, a small group of climbers, with limited resources, can mount a successful climb. The expansion and advent of alpine style climbs by small groups in remote areas and on difficult routes opened the doors to more ascents by extraordinarily talented mountaineers. By the late 1970s, more complex routes and lines were being climbed, and climbed faster.

In one sense, climbers on an alpine style ascent are more at risk as there are no fixed ropes that can be used in both good and bad weather for ascent or descent. There are no series of camps, stocked or unstocked, to retreat to in the case of bad weather or illness, or to advance to with a light load to save energy. With no fixed camps, if there is an injury, sudden bad weather or unexpected delays, the team could be forced to bivy in extreme situations or places. On the other side, by carrying less food and equipment, a team can move faster and, moving faster, will be on the mountain for less time, and be on dangerous parts of their route for shorter periods. This is an important factor when weather plays a hand or when moving through areas prone to avalanche or rock fall. There is a downside to moving too fast on big mountains though. Rapid gains in altitude must be balanced by superior conditioning and perhaps more time at a lower camp before a dash to the summit. In expedition style climbing, the whole process of ferrying loads and advancing camps almost guarantees sufficient time for acclimatization. By moving faster, and in today's world of adventure climbing – depending on professional organizers to stock camps and move logistics – it is quite possible to over climb one's acclimatization profile and succumb to acute mountain sickness, high-altitude pulmonary edema or worse.

In an alpine style ascent, typically everyone goes to the summit, or no one goes. With less reliance on porters, or other members of the team to ferry loads and stock a camp site, there is more emphasis on the individual, and more of an individual challenge. The smaller the group, the more the emphasis is on the individual. The extension of that is the solo ascent.

There is also a more esoteric appeal: the purity of the climb. I, along with some others, feel that a climb is not so much about a public celebration of standing on the summit, but is rather a private, personal accomplishment. Some extraordinary climbers of today feel that the individual experience of a new route or climb that has not been done before can be spoiled if done in a group setting or even by taking along a photographer. Alpine style climbing became the new mainstream challenge.

And in 1979, the South Face of Aconcagua had yet to be climbed alpine style. Naturally, that appealed to us greatly.

By deciding to do an alpine style ascent, carrying everything with us as we ascended, with no fixed lines or camps to stage from or retreat to, we committed to a rather extreme project.

As we prepared, we became aware of another group of three American climbers, all from California, also planning an expedition to the South Face but who were about two months ahead of us in schedule. They were going to attempt the original French line of ascent.

And they were going to attempt it alpine style.

Ed Connor, the team leader, Guy Andrews and Chuck Bludworth set off from their base camp in Plaza Francia at the end of December 1979, and in January 1980, reached the summit ridge via the French Route. Climbing conditions were terrible, fierce. Pinned down in a ferocious storm by the notorious "viento blanco" (white wind), they struggled desperately to survive for two days before attempting the last 250 yards to the summit. Connor made it and survived, Bludworth and Andrews did not.

Suffering from frostbite, malnutrition and extreme exhaustion, Connor was able to crawl to Refugio Independencia, (a high camp at 21,450 feet with limited shelter and the ruins of a stone hut) to wait out the storm and then descended further to a climbers' hut. From there, he was aided down the mountain by Venezuelan mountaineers who had climbed from the other side of the mountain. ("Land of the White Wind" by Sam Moses in the April 14, 1980 issue of *Sports Illustrated* is an excellent article about their climb. And, Connor briefly records their climb in an American Alpine Journal publication of 1981.)

Today, there are slightly more than a dozen routes and variations on the South Face. In 1979 there was one, with one variant. In the bold 1954 expedition, the French team of world class climbers pioneered the route that to this day, remains a classic line on the Face. In 1974, Rheinhold Messner, from Italy, climbing with an expedition on the French Route, departed from their high camp and soloed a previously unclimbed variant to the summit. He descended back to the high camp and then with remaining team members descended to the foot of the Face.

Because all ascents up to 1979 had been expedition style, they took between three weeks to a month on the Face itself. By climbing with less equipment, food and fuel, Connor, Andrews and Bludworth reached the summit ridge in seven days and then another two before Connor was able to summit.

We were hoping for an ascent of about five to six days once on the Face proper. For amateur climbers with little big mountain experience, this was pretty bold. In fact, it was brash. But we thought it was very doable if the weather and climbing conditions cooperated.

As a side note, to illustrate how climbing progressed in just a few short years, in 1990, Thomas Bubendorfer of Austria, after nearly two weeks of on-site route study, training and conditioning at the foot of the wall, in near perfect conditions and with good weather, solo climbed the South Face in an astonishing 15 hours and 30 minutes. He carried only basic climbing tools, no rope, no tent or bivy gear and only minimum clothing and food.

Go light, go fast.

2

Gear Selection and Training

If there is one thing that makes the difference between climbs of today and those of twenty, thirty, forty or more years ago, it would be gear and equipment. It is hard to underestimate the benefits of modern, functional, efficient, lightweight clothing, gear and equipment.

Go light, go fast.

You might think that selecting gear for a high altitude climbing expedition would be straightforward. Well, in some sense of the word, it is. But in 1979, equipment selection was a far cry from what is commonly available today. For example, Gore-Tex clothing was in its infancy. It was developing rapidly but not completely refined nor widely distributed, the seams often leaked, and it was a bit pricey at the time.

We were very much on a budget, and we had no sponsors, no backers, no real patrons. Brian and I were able to use some of the gear provided to us by our profession as PJs. Hugh didn't have that luxury. Most, if not all, of the clothing and equipment available was bulkier, heavier and less efficient than that in use today. Of course, the same could be said for what we were planning on using in 1980 in comparison to the clothing, climbing paraphernalia and equipment used by the French team of 1954. Knowing that we had lighter and 'better' clothing, gear and equipment helped give us the confidence that we could do the climb lighter and therefore faster.

Brian and I had many, many discussions over the phone about clothing, climbing gear, tentage, ropes, stoves and fuel, what could serve as a double duty item, and what might be frivolous or for base camp only. As Brian was the leader, I ended up defaulting to him for final decisions on all team climbing items such as ropes, pitons, ice screws, snow-flukes and equipment like the tent, stove, etc. This was actually easy to do as we were pretty much in sync. Each of us was then responsible for our own clothing and personal equipment. Clothing turned out to be not too difficult a decision. For the most part, we had decent climbing wear that just needed to be tweaked a bit. Plus, some of the really nice, high end items were usually too expensive for us, so we simply went with what we had.

The one item I did, however, spend long hours researching was boots – boots suitable for high altitude, cold, alpine climbing. Boots you could rock climb in, trudge through snow in, put crampons on, and that would keep your feet warm above 20,000 feet.

On Denali I had used "bunny boots" or "Mickey Mouse" boots – slang for the military's extreme cold, vapor barrier boots. Originally developed for the Korean conflict, they were great in level or soft snow, and they did keep your feet warm. With flexible lace-up crampons of the day, they were okay for most snow trekking and easy technical ice climbing. However, climbing on rock and high angle snow or ice was not going to be possible with those.

The climbing boots I was using for work (Lowa Civettas – the 1970s leather edition) were excellent for peaks in the Northwest such as Mt. Hood, Mt. Rainier, the Three Sisters, etc., but not suitable for the cold expected at over 18,000 feet. So, I needed to obtain what other high altitude mountaineers had been using for years.

One of the best high altitude mountaineering boots of the day was the Lowa Triplex. General construction of high-quality climbing and mountaineering boots was similar across the brands, but the quality and materials used sometimes differed slightly. The Lowa Triplex was a big, heavy, leather, three-piece boot with a nice Vibram (specialized rubber) sole. It was a very rigid boot with excellent stiffness provided by a full-length shank in the midsole. The outer boot was a heavy leather shell. The mid, or inner boot, was a lace-up, high-top shoe of soft, smooth leather with a thin smooth leather sole. The innermost layer was a thick felt sock affair for insulation. Of course, once the felt inner was wet, it pretty much lost its insulation value. But then if you were using Triplex boots, you were expecting the temperatures to be below freezing and not to be wading in water. Between the inner shank and the Vibram bottom sole was a plastic/nylon mid-sole plate to give the boot lateral and torsional stiffness. The outer Vibram sole was glued to the plastic mid-sole, and the Vibram sole was stitched at the welt to the upper shell using a very tough nylon/polyester thread. They weighed about seven pounds for the pair. Then you needed to wear a boot gaiter or lower leg covering that went over your boot and part way up your leg, designed to keep snow out of the boot. That added almost another pound for both legs.

I sought out a couple of climbers I knew who had Triplex boots that I was able to look at, touch and feel. I was definitely not happy with their bulk and weight. Not wanting to be encumbered by the weight of the Triplex, I continued to research boots and eventually found a brand new release. It was a double boot with high tech aluminized layers embedded in the outer shell, also with a wooden shank to provide stiffness with light weight and to reduce heat conduction, and a form fitted Aveolite (aluminized closed cell foam) liner as the inner boot. It was about two thirds the weight of the Triplex.

I'm thinking, *go light, go fast*, and I bought a pair as fast as I could. Brian and Hugh were less than impressed, but more on that later.

Today, boots such as the Scarpa Inverno, Scarpa Phantom 6000/8000, the Lowa Expedition 6000/8000, or the La Sportiva Olympus Mons are the standard for high altitude climbing. They are typically double boots with high tech materials throughout, a type of Aveolite liner with multi-layer aluminized cloth to provide cushioning and to reflect heat back into the boot. All come with built in gaiters and weigh between three and a half to a little over five pounds.

Anyway, with boots obtained, I turned to crampon selection. My new boots would accept either a new at the time rigid style crampon with a step-in binding or the traditional lace-on/strap-on rigid crampons common of the day. Since I had never used the newer style crampons and Brian and Hugh were using high quality, rigid crampons with lace-on bindings, I followed suit. There is a significant downside of a crampon with a lace-on binding, however. To insure minimum, or zero, independent movement of the crampon in relation to the boot, one must tighten the laces – as in nice and tight – with a tendency to restrict circulation in the foot. Not good.

Somewhere in the middle of one of my phone discussions with Brian, I thought about food – probably right before lunch one day. Brian and I didn't spend too much time discussing food, though in hindsight we should have. For work, i.e., being in the field, we were both I'll-eat-anything-that-isn't-moving kind of guys. It was all about the calories being enough to keep you going.

Brian relayed that the pile of team gear was growing in size, and he feared that "too much" food would put us into trouble, bulk wise. Since there were three of us, we only had three packs to put everything in. Everything – personal gear, climbing gear, ropes, tent, stove, fuel, clothing, sleeping bags and so on – had to fit. He was afraid that with too much, everything would literally not go into our packs. The idea of eliminating one of our ropes or another piece of team climbing gear was a non-starter, so we revisited the menu. We calculated again the number of days we expected to be at base camp, then on the mountain actually climbing, then the descent. Next, we added three days for a reserve, an emergency or bad weather. Since we were thinking we could do the climb in five to six days, and descend in one, that gave us a target of carrying enough meals for nine to ten days.

We decided early on that we wanted freeze dried meals. They had worked well for us in the past and were a staple amongst climbers, trekkers and adventurers – essentially for anyone who wanted to go light. Later, in yet another conversation, Brian said he had looked at the number of calories listed on an individual meal package. He had determined that for our main meal – usually in the evening – the three of us could share two jumbo sized meal packets...and he proceeded to tell me how.

I somehow bought into the idea. What was I thinking?

Afterwards, with the revised menu plan, Brian told me he had removed about one third of the food from the pile and suddenly it looked okay!

For our tent, Brian had selected a high end, four-season, mountaineering expedition model by, I believe, Bibler. (Bibler's designs were later acquired by Black Diamond.) The only modification we made to the tent was to add three or four, 12-inch long, one-inch wide webbing straps or runners, sewn through from the outside of the tent to the inside of the tent at the seam of the wall and floor. The idea was so that you could tie or clip the tent into protection on the outside and then clip yourself into the other end of the webbing while inside the tent. Of course, we (at least I) did not anticipate ever needing to use this feature…

With the gear selection and food situation squared away, at some point I realized that I needed to step up my game training wise.

In preparing for the McKinley/Denali climb I had been doing quite a bit of mountain running in SoCal, mostly at or above 9,000 feet. I had an older friend – a training mentor and bicycling and trekking buddy – Cliff Cummings. Cliff was in phenomenal shape and together we had road biked, hiked and ran a number of trails throughout SoCal. One of our favorite run/hikes was Rabbit Peak on the edge of Anza Borrego. We used it as a gauge of our fitness level before doing ascents of the north face of San Jacinto Peak (via Snow Creek).

Rabbit Peak is regarded as a difficult, very strenuous hike in Southern California due to its vertical rise of 6,700 feet, its remoteness and the desert topography. It is about 16 miles round trip. We would start just below sea level near the Salton Sea a little before dawn at 5:30 a.m. and haul ass to the summit. We usually cached a couple of liters of water about halfway up to save weight and were always very motivated to find the cache on the way down.

We'd normally be back in Palm Desert by 3 p.m., having a much-needed beer. (For anyone interested, our fastest ascent was on February 28, 1976, in three hours and nine minutes from the trailhead at Fillmore Street in Oasis in the Coachella Valley.)

We considered Rabbit Peak as a suitable training hike for Snow Creek, on the north side of Mt. San Jacinto (10,834 feet).

The north face of Mt. San Jacinto via Snow Creek is regarded as the steepest uninterrupted rise in the continental U.S. with 10,000 vertical feet in less than five miles. The ascent begins in the desert and finishes in an alpine environment on the summit. Although not technically difficult, it is regarded by many as one of the premier ascents in Southern California. Most people who climb it take two days.

On April 3, 1976, Cliff, another friend named Ralph Glen and I had near perfect weather and excellent climbing conditions and decided to do Snow Creek. Cliff and I made the ascent in just under six hours (from the watershed caretakers' hut to the summit), with Ralph about 45 minutes behind.

Now, a little more than three years later, I was concerned about the upcoming project in South America as my level of fitness was not up to the same standard as when I was training for Denali. It was more difficult to train in Portland for several reasons including more job responsibility and adverse weather. There was no way I could train at the same level as when I was in SoCal. So, I upped my running program, did more calisthenics and ventured into the hills whenever I could, hoping for the best.

In addition to the training, there was one major hurdle I had to address before the end of the year. I needed to obtain approval for a month's leave (vacation) from work. I had the vacation time available, but the normally accepted maximum time away from work was about two weeks. After several different conversations, I managed to convince my boss, the squadron's Operations Officer and then his boss, the Squadron Commander, to allow me the consecutive days off. They agreed but mentioned that they expected me to accompany the unit for an upcoming deployment. Of course, I said yes.

In the last quarter of 1979, the 304th ARRSq was selected to augment the USAF Rescue Squadron at Plattsburgh AFB, New York. The mission was to provide aeromedical coverage and emergency evacuation for the 1980 Winter

Olympic Games taking place in Lake Placid, New York, from February 13-24, 1980. In January 1980, we deployed via a USAF C-5, with a small number of helicopters and personnel to Plattsburgh AFB and began flying orientation, training and rescue missions. The helicopters and a few unit members went early and the helicopters would stay throughout the three to four week deployment. Most of the squadron personnel would rotate in and out for two weeks of duty. There was no shortage of people who wanted to be there for the games themselves, but not so many for the transport and initial set up phase. That allowed me to deploy with the unit, coordinate with local area medical personnel and to look at hospitals and landing zones. Then I added my comments to existing protocols and procedures and returned to Portland some 12 hours before my flight to meet Brian and Hugh – home in the late afternoon, with barely enough time to wash clothes, repack and make ready for the next morning's flight.

Brian, Hugh and several other folks picked me up at the airport in El Paso, Texas, and we drove to Holloman AFB, near Alamogordo, New Mexico. This was my first time meeting Hugh. He was younger, a little taller than me, (I'm short at 5 feet 8 inches), looked fit, congenial and had a quick British wit (he was British after all). According to Brian, Hugh was a rock jock – a wizard on technical rock. That ability could prove extremely valuable on our attempt. He had experience in typical British (atrocious) weather and was strong and fit. And, though he didn't have much experience at high altitude, on snow and ice or on big mountains, he and Brian had gone to Mexico and climbed the volcano Popocatepetl in December 1979. Brian related to me that Hugh had done a great job, and had no issues related to the altitude of the climb. I had a good 'vibe' or feeling from Hugh and was looking forward to getting to know him on our climb.

Even though Hugh didn't have much experience on snow and ice, Brian felt the three of us were a good complement to one another. After dinner, we set to the task of final preparation and packing of our travel bags. In those days, travel was much easier and the world more trusting. We packed everything in our military, canvas tactical gear bags, including several dozens of iso-butane gas cylinders for our stoves, wrapping them in a couple of sleeping bags. Everything would go as baggage. No problem.

Well, just one small problem. Brian and Hugh each had (very) nice small SLR cameras, as did I. Theirs were Leicas, mine was an Olympus OM-2. And, I had a Kodak Pocket Instamatic in 110 format. Brian was insistent that we take just two cameras in order to save weight – and that we take the Leicas. I argued the point vociferously but to no avail. Eventually I agreed to put my SLR to the side, to be picked up upon return. But I would not relinquish my pocket camera, explaining that it would not leave my pocket, they didn't need to worry about its weight, and thus it would be on the summit with me if all else went to hell. They agreed on that condition.

And off we went to rest for the night and our flights the next day.

3

Getting There

O ur flights were long, and I was reminded just how far Santiago, Chile is from the U.S.! Of course, we had tried to schedule our flights too closely and as our aircraft arrived at the gate in Santiago, we could see our connecting flight to Mendoza, Argentina taxiing away. Missing our flight from Santiago to Mendoza definitely put a crimp in our plans – certainly in my plans anyway.

Enter "Bolivian Al"...

We were somewhere on the sidewalk outside the passenger arrival area in Santiago when Brian and Hugh went off to see what they could do about getting us back on track. I was a bit grumpy at this point and was happy all I had to do was watch our gear and luggage. After a while Brian and Hugh showed back up and soon thereafter a beat-up pickup truck pulled to the curb. Brian entered into a broken Spanglish pantomime with the driver – Al from Bolivia – while I stood by not fully comprehending what was being arranged.

In short order, Brian turned and said, "Okay, he's going to take us to Mendoza – load up. Oh, and by the way, since I'm the leader you two are in back." We loaded everything in the bed of the pickup and made ready for the 200+ mile, cross-Andes drive.

After some hours I noticed we were traveling quite slowly, it was sunset and we were passing the entrance to the ski resort of Portillo, Chile. Not far to the border. The pickup was laboring with the altitude – now approaching 10,500 feet – but all was well. I kept bouncing back and forth and side to side, but securely wedged in between our gear, Hugh and Bolivian Al's cargo. Through the tunnel and over the top, and now downhill to Mendoza.

But, not quite so fast. We passed a small Army outpost at the actual border and then about an hour before Mendoza, we stopped at the Argentinian customs border control checkpoint. There, we were directed to take all the gear out of the truck. Al was instructed by the Argentinian Army and customs officials to move his truck to one side behind several other vehicles. We figured out the customs checkpoint was closed for the night.

We arranged three six by two-foot spaces on the concrete pad next to the customs shed (Bolivian Al slept in his truck) and spent the night sleeping on top of the gear. There was no restaurant or snack shop so of course, no meals. Early the next morning we needed to move everything to the side to avoid being stepped on by the customs officials, and I finally asked Brian, "So, what's up?" Brian replied that apparently Bolivian Al didn't have one of the right forms for the truck. We were free to go, but the truck wasn't. We needed to find another vehicle to take us to Mendoza.

Brian's journal notes about that night and the following day, onward to our next destination, Mendoza:

"...our first night in South America spent on the ground in a remote Customs outpost in the Andes. A few hours of Spanish practice on some local militaries guarding the border, we share the warmth of their fire which consists of a few lumps of coal burning on the street and retire to the parking lot exhausted from a day so long we no longer remembered its beginning. By daybreak cars, maybe 100 in all, were already lined up to make early starts to cross the border frontier. Probably headed to the Chilean coast we theorized. More importantly, we hoped the situation might be reversed on the Chilean side. We estimated that by 10:00 a.m. the first wave should arrive. By 9:00 a.m. a Ford pickup, the first to pull into the site.

We sent our 'best man' (Al) to have a look under the canvas camper to see if there was room and then try to persuade the driver to take us to Mendoza. But alas, the vehicle had not come from Chile, but from a tunnel work site just this side of the border itself - and its cargo, the victim of a fatal accident, just lay in the bed of the pickup without comment. By noon the traffic started to pour through our home away from home. It was an impossible situation trying to find a vehicle capable of carrying the four of us and our bags. By 1:00 p.m., we were able to contract a truck from Uspallata, a village about halfway between where we were and Mendoza to come for us. We were finally on the road again. First stop, the home of Bolivian Al's family. A very generous invitation was difficult to refuse, but we had to be on our way."

We end up at the Hotel Ritz – not of the Ritz Carlton franchise and definitely more cost friendly for a group of budget-minded climbers. Shortly after arrival we are sitting out front, writing post cards, talking about the morrow, looking at women pass by and thinking about the climb.

Brian's journal continues:

"...The hotel was a quiet place on Peru Avenue, chairs out front provided us a place to relax and watch the parade of street traffic and pedestrians. After our respective turns in the shower, we awaited the arrival of our agent, Rudy Parra, the head of the local Mountaineering Association with instructions for us for the execution of climbing permit application.

Meanwhile we had time to scribble out a few post cards. Rudy finally arrived, there was a cursory check of our equipment by the 'Big Chief' of the Mountaineering Association, more I think to find out what we had to sell than anything. The hotel management incidentally did not respond very well to seeing their lobby rearranged by nearly 350 pounds of climbing gear. We chalked it up to a lack of a sense of humor.

The easy part of the permit application now finished, we set out trying to finish as much paper pushing as possible before the offices closed for the weekend.

We settled back into our hotel for the remainder of the weekend and continuously re-computed our monetary situation. Things in Argentina were very expensive, and the delays were cutting quite deeply into our low budget. The only redeeming value of being stuck in Mendoza for the weekend was the large collection of absolutely stunning ladies. Young, slim, dark eyes, and just generally erotica maxima. This fantasy-come-true soon ended Monday morning as we set back about the business of processing the remaining paperwork necessary to obtain our permit. The police doctor, having reviewed our EKGs, sent us onto the identification section (long wait), prints, photos, background questions and then to the military post for an instant replay of the police procedures. What a pleasant day dragging around Mendoza like sweltering dogs. Just one thing left, a return trip to the 'Bomberos' (Fire and Rescue Service) for the elusive final clearance – and the entry of our names into the official log. What a thrill to read the names of some of the great climbers here before us: Messner, Uremura, Genet, etc. We paused with a chill running from head to toe and entered our names and the words "Ruta Sur Messner." The room went quiet, for only six weeks earlier, three just like ourselves set out in much the same way, just one returned."

Mendoza, Argentina

We were entranced by the beauty of the city and its inhabitants (okay... the women, and there were lots of beautiful women...). We found the politeness of the people warming and were enthralled by the rhythm of life. It was both vibrant and laid back. We particularly liked the custom of 'Once' (*ohn-seh*) or 'Merienda'. This, we learned, was a late afternoon tea/coffee/snack affair that one needed to partake in to be able to survive until dinner, which was usually about 10 or 11 p.m.

In those days you needed a permit to climb Aconcagua. You couldn't just show up at the mountain and begin to climb. Of course, there was no one at the trailhead at that time to stop you from doing so if you chose not to get the permit – no ranger station, no check in, no on-site registration.

So, the city of Mendoza was where we needed to start the process, register for the climb and obtain the necessary permits. Of course, being a couple of days late thanks to missing a flight and an unexpected night in a remote parking lot, the offices we needed to check in with were closed for the weekend. Well, truth be told, there were worse places where one could have been derailed.

One of the things we did accomplish was a visit by and chat with Rudy Parra. Rudy was a climber, a police official and the founder and head of the local mountaineering association. He detailed the process of obtaining our climbing permit and gave us a letter of introduction to a colleague of his, Fernando Grajales, a legendary Argentinean climber. Fernando ran a rustic lodge and ski center right at the entrance to the Aconcagua massif. Today, Parra's "Aconcagua Trek" and Fernando's "Grajales Expeditions" are among the best known guide and expedition services for those wanting to climb Aconcagua or trek in the region.

The following Monday we started our rounds of the various offices in the city. We were getting poked, prodded, questioned, had our fingerprints taken, and IDs recorded. All was going more or less smoothly until the last office. There was the normal chatter of people returning to work after a weekend – until they heard of our intended route. The office came to a quiet standstill as everyone was now paying attention. It was the proverbial 'you could hear a pin drop' moment. Once it was clear that we were serious and planning an attempt on the South Face, they asked if we were aware that two Americans had died only two months before on the Face.

We replied that we did, and in fact had spoken with Ed Connor, the expedition leader who had summited and survived. We signed in the same registration book that previous teams had. Most of the names were unknown to us and almost all had registered for the standard routes. Some names were icons in the climbing world. It was fascinating and humbling to see the names and signatures of famous mountaineers such as Rheinhold Messner, Ray Genet, Naomi Uemura and others. Along with the team of Connor, Bludworth and Andrews, we noticed a couple of other teams that had also registered for the South Face after Connor's. Asking about these other groups, the authorities related they had bailed due to extremely bad weather and heavy snowfall, making for serious avalanche hazard.

For a few fleeting moments it appeared that we might not be granted permission. That was something we had not contemplated. Eventually, they did grant approval though it was obvious they were concerned about the outcome. There were a couple of provisions, however: We ended up needing to put down a "rescue deposit" that we (I, anyway) were not planning on, apparently as a result of the conditions on the mountain that season and the fact that we were attempting the South Face. Our already meager funds took another hit. And we were instructed to head to an Army base with a hospital where they would administer a fitness test including a stint on a treadmill hooked up to a cardiac monitor. I didn't know if all this was normal or not – but by now they had my attention about how serious they were taking our project. Presumably we passed the fitness eval, or maybe they just wanted to be able to tell our surviving relatives about the care they had taken.

In any event, we were now headed back west toward where we had spent the first night in Argentina. From there we would head just a little north to the entrance of the Horcones River Valley. Then into Fernando's aforementioned ski lodge.

Fernando had climbed in the Himalayas and had been a member of a pioneering climb and first ascent of Aconcagua's West side via the Southwest Ridge in January 1953. This route emerges first on the South summit and then via the Guanaco Ridge to the mountain's highest point, the North summit. It is one of the longest routes on the mountain. Other climbers on that first ascent were Francisco Ibanez, F. Marmillod and his wife.

A revered figure in Argentinian climbing circles, Fernando had our complete attention and welcomed us into his lodge, making us feel at home. He was quite enthused – and concerned – about our plan to attempt the South Face direct.

After a truly good night's sleep, the next morning we – mostly Brian – arranged for mules to take our gear, food and all base camp equipment to Plaza Francia, the base camp area at the foot of the Face. We would carry relatively lightly loaded packs and hike in as part of conditioning. Departure was set for the following day.

Fernando wanted to see our gear so of course we showed it to him. He nodded about how gear had improved since his day, and all was going well…until he saw my boots. To say he disapproved of my selection would be putting it mildly. Brian and Hugh looked off in the distance; they had tried the same arguments Fernando was making. The only thing was this was Fernando Grajales talking. He had actually been on the mountain, had summited, and had seen dozens of climbers pass through his lodge.

He then offered me the use of his personal triplex climbing boots. Hugh and Brian were now paying attention. I waffled, not wanting to offend him, so he dug them out of storage. They were ten or so years old at that point but looked to be in excellent condition. They were not Lowas – I don't remember the brand – but the outer shell had adjustable buckles, the second or inner boot was a lace up one very similar to the Lowa and there was the standard felt innermost layer. Fernando swore by them. And was insistent that I use those and not mine. Mostly to appease them all, I agreed to use Fernando's boots, but only if they fit. Never in a million years would I have thought they would fit… I tried them on. And they fit like a glove – perfectly! Now I was in a conundrum but decided to go with the majority.

What, I wondered, had happened to *"go light, go fast"*?

Off to bed relatively early, each of us thinking about the mountain, the route, and what we were attempting.

And then we're up bright and early and stumble in for breakfast and our thoughts are on the day ahead.

February 20, 1980, Brian's diary notes:

> *"We woke to a perfect warm day, loaded our sacks into Fernando's truck, waved our goodbyes to the staff and set out on our dream. From this point on everything was a carefully detailed plan that would allow no deviation. Our first task: we must set our camp and wait the time it would take to acclimatize.*
>
> *The walk in went more quickly than we had imagined. The Arrieros (muleteers) with their mules who had started from Cruz de Caña caught up with us near Confluencia where the two branches of the Horcones River join. Mike and I, sensing an opportunity to really exhaust ourselves tried to keep up with the four-legged cargo conveyors. Those mules can walk! I thought Mike must have the jawbone of an asshole to even suggest such a tormenting scheme, but we were able to maintain pace with them over the next few*

hours and arrived at Plaza Francia, our base camp, not far behind. Hugh, acting much more sensible, opted for a slow easy pace and arrived sometime later. In all, it had taken just seven and a half hours to cover the 18 miles and 4,000 feet of rise. With our equipment having been deposited on the ground by the Arrieros, we set about not building up our base camp as we theorized every other party had probably done, but instead located our floppy flyer (an REI collapsible Frisbee like thing) and chased it around in the cold thin air of our 12,000-foot base camp site. Truly a wonderful device, it actually to our delight, flew better at altitude! As the temperature began to drop in the late afternoon, the Arrieros mounted their horses and led their mules down the same path we had all just walked.

As they rounded the last corner out of our sight, we each, I am sure in his own way, wondered when we would next see another human face. The task of setting the base camp up did not take long and once complete left us time that evening to admire our objective and examine the route through our 150 mm camera lens.

Our hike to Plaza Francia started well and we soon found ourselves alone on the journey, the muleteers and their mules had not yet caught up with us. There was no one else on the trail that day, ascending or descending. The terrain was magnificent, the colors resplendent with small green ground cover, tints of ochre on the hillsides and soon the dirty white of snowpack and ice on the river. The valley was beautiful, between a mile and a half mile wide, sometimes more, sometimes less. The riverbed filled much of the valley, though the river itself was usually confined to a small channel near the middle, and sometimes braided. There were no constructed bridges over the river in 1980, no buildings, no trail posts, no markers of any kind. We crossed the river where we thought we should, often on enormous ice bridges, wondering if they would be there on our return.

We came to one particular turn in the valley, and as hundreds before us and thousands after us have, we stopped in disbelief. The mountain massif and the South Face, mostly hidden by the Horcones River Valley walls until then, was suddenly and dramatically revealed.

My heart leapt into my throat. *How am I ever going to climb **that**?*

Before too long the mule train caught up with us and more joking than serious, I suggested to Brian that we should pace it, or even beat the mules to base camp. To my dismay, he agreed, and I had no other choice. As we adjusted our pace, I flashed back to the time on Denali when I was ferrying a huge load from one low camp to the next higher one and a really attractive female climber with a day pack slowly overtook me and I was stupid enough to increase my pace and begin a conversation. I managed to stay with her for about five minutes and then she just smiled and stepped it up...

Hugh simply laughed and said he'd see us there. The relaxed trek to Plaza Francia suddenly disappeared. As we climbed higher, the green hues disappeared and eventually only the orange brownish yellow of the hillsides and the hundreds of tones of black and white remained.

We didn't beat the mules into Plaza Francia but were not far behind. We helped the muleteers unload our gear and then paused for a bit, wanting to relax in the remaining hours of the afternoon. I dug out this little frisbee thing from REI and began tossing it back and forth with Brian, figuring we had plenty of time that afternoon to erect the tent and days to organize our gear.

Top: Hugh enjoying the sights of Mendoza. Bottom: The author, at left, with Brian (photo by Hugh Grandfield).

February 1980: Cruz de Caña.

February 1980: Fernando's Lodge.

Brian and the author, hoping the ice bridge doesn't collapse (photo by Hugh Grandfield).

The author and Brian once the mountain and the intimidating South Face came into full view, stopping them in their tracks (photo by Hugh Grandfield).

Top: Brian and the author, beginning to step it up to pace the mules. Bottom: The approach – Upper Horcones River Valley. For perspective, Brian and the author are the small, dark figures in the lower right corner of the image (photos by Hugh Grandfield).

Passing the time at Base Camp with the "floppy flyer" (photo by Hugh Grandfield).

Top: The awe-inspiring South Face of Aconcagua. Bottom: The South Face alight in afternoon alpen-glow.

4

Base Camp, Plaza Francia

B ase camp was a magnificent place. Situated just off and above the glacier moraine on tierra firma, Plaza Francia has a commanding view of the spectacular setting. Down valley, the Inferior Horcones River wanders toward Confluencia, where the drainages of the Inferior and Superior Horcones Rivers meet to form a bigger stream. Up valley is the head of the glacier and about two miles distant from our tent, the South Face rises abruptly and vertically in a huge arc. The South Face absolutely dominates the area and being as close as we were, the higher elevations were foreshortened, making accurate estimation of distance and height difficult. The south and north summits were clearly visible, as is the Guanaco Ridge.

As in any high mountain setting, the zone we were in was mostly sterile, literally with little to no plant life and figuratively with no green or green shades, but a lot of deep brown and black and white and many tones in between. The late afternoon sun brought out spectacular contrasts with deep shadows, sometimes flaming and sometimes soft golden alpen-glow on the face, and occasionally seemed to turn the air itself into a purplish, almost magenta, tint. Surrounding us, save the Inferior Horcones Glacier and its track, were peaks and ridgelines. From base camp, our route via the central pillar defines the Face and was (and in my opinion, remains) the classic line on this 9,000 vertical foot wall. We were the only souls for miles around; ours the only tent. It was to be our home for about a week and a half.

We needed to stay in Base Camp for a minimum of 10 days in order to properly acclimatize to the increase in altitude. Plaza Francia is about 13,700 feet above sea level and the air is noticeably thinner than at sea level. Although the ratio of oxygen in the air is the same as at sea level, there is much less of it. With the decrease in the partial pressure of oxygen in the atmosphere – in the air you breathe – your body senses the need for more oxygen. There are several compensatory actions by your body, but the best one: it goes into overdrive to increase the number of circulating red blood cells. The kidneys release a hormone that causes the bone marrow to produce more red blood cells. To make room for the increased number of red blood cells in your circulatory system your urine output increases, pulling fluid from the circulatory system and your body moves fluid from the circulatory system into (primarily) the lungs and the cranial spaces. Most of the excess fluid in your lungs and cranial vault is re-absorbed. When it's not, especially if you climb too high too fast, you run the increased risk of high altitude pulmonary edema and high altitude cerebral edema.

This acclimatization is a finite, physiological process. Each individual is a little different, but the process is usually triggered by an increase in elevation above 5,000-6,000 feet for a couple of days or more. Once triggered, the bulk of adaption or acclimatization normally occurs in three to four weeks, with the greatest part of that in the first two weeks. In the best-case scenario, as you climb, you typically stay just ahead of the acclimation process, always in a little deficit, always keeping the trigger pressed. Again, it is an individual process, but the vast majority of people cannot acclimate any higher than about 18,000 feet. Once your body and individual physiology are acclimated to that height and the partial pressure of oxygen present, if you go higher your body will begin to work without sufficient oxygen. Subtle and not so subtle changes occur. Some individuals can function almost normally (save sustained aerobic effort), others exhibit mood swings or departures from their norm, changes in metabolizing food, weight loss, judgement, and so on. Climb higher and everyone exhibits those symptoms. Climb even higher, and the partial pressure of oxygen present in the air you breathe is not sufficient to keep all of your brain cells alive – again, different for different individuals, but generally this begins between 24,000 and 26,000 feet and continues on up (the death zone). That is why almost everyone who climbs above 26,000 feet uses oxygen. Without it, you will lose brain cells and it becomes a question of how many.

Without supplemental oxygen, the faster you go, the fewer you lose.

Go light, go fast.

So in general, if you live at or near sea-level, climb or travel to any altitude above 8,000 feet and you push too high too fast you become more susceptible to acute mountain sickness, high altitude pulmonary edema or high altitude cerebral edema.

Since we came from near sea level in the U.S., as soon as we reached Fernando's lodge at Cruz de Caña, we essentially began our adaptation, and we would do our time in base camp.

We fell into a loose daily rhythm, generated by the mountain, the rising and setting of the sun, and our own energy levels. We tried to get a feel for what was in store. The first day was an organization and sorting day. We separated the gear and equipment into base camp-only stuff, our own individual items, climbing gear and equipment for the Face, and food. Anything that was not going with us on the Face would be taken down to Confluencia in about a week and cached, to wait for us to pick up on our return. In the mornings we collected snow to melt for water, prepared lunch and separated out the evening's meal. Beginning on day three or four we began to venture out for conditioning hikes and to try to keep our legs in shape.

One morning at about 7:30 a.m., we were startled by what sounded like a muted sonic boom, or explosion, but of a much lower frequency, something you feel in your stomach. I'm not sure who realized it first, but we were suddenly aware there was an avalanche of massive size on the Face. We opened the tent and looked up valley.

We were stunned.

A section of the second or upper glacier about a half mile wide and two hundred feet high had fractured off and impacted upon the lower glacier below. There was an immense amount of boiling snow and ice rushing down the Face. I mentally noted that the central pillar itself, as well as the face of the promontory and its left-hand side looked mostly clear from the track of the avalanche. It appeared that everything in the wide couloir to the right, including the right-hand side of the promontory itself, was on the edge of the track. From our vantage point though, especially with the cloud of snow, it was difficult to judge the edges of the track and the run-out zone.

Spellbound, we watched until it reached the bottom about two miles away. Several minutes went by and then the tent fluttered in the pressure wave from the falling mass of snow and ice.

The mountain had announced it was in control, and while we might be permitted on the peak and summit, it would not be a conquest. The idea of "conquering" a mountain is really a misnomer – mostly an invention of the press.

One may climb or ascend or stand on the summit of a mountain, but one does not "conquer" the mountain.

On one of our later conditioning hikes, we went to the base of the wall for a recce (reconnaissance) and to pre-position some of our climbing gear so the trek to the foot of the Face with all the camp gear would be just a little easier. In scouting the terrain, we decided we would put in an advance base camp and move to it one or two days before launching on the climb itself.

I decided during that recce and after witnessing the avalanche of a few days before, that we would not take the start of the French Route to the right of the promontory, but rather a snow, rock, and ice gully on its left-hand side. There was just too much stuff coming down the big couloir. Looking up from the site of our advance base camp, it appeared that once we were nearly level with the top of the promontory, we should be able to transition to our right and gain the central rib itself.

On several mornings, collecting snow close to the tent became problematic. Occasionally, there was not much new snowfall in base camp and the existing snow and ice were very dirty. We ended up ranging out to almost half a mile just to collect barely enough to make water for the day. *Well, better than the desert with nothing*, I thought.

Apart from collecting snow, personal contemplation time and our daily hikes, we ate. We had fortified our base camp meals with some staples and food we had purchased in Mendoza, which turned out to be a wise decision.

By this point, Brian and Hugh had begun a low-level bickering campaign with one another. The comments were sometimes amusing, sometimes acrimonious. This, I hoped, was a result of our self-imposed requirement to stay in place and the resulting frustration of not making any progress upward.

Brian describes our time in base camp in his journal notes:

> *The Marque de Sade himself could not have devised a more demonic punishment than to have to wait in a base camp at the foot of your desired objective while your body slowly produces enough hemoglobin to allow you to function at high elevations. Just spinning our wheels, living on a very small daily subsistence ration day after day hassling with water, which there never seemed to be enough of, going outside for a walk until the sun, made more intense by lack of atmosphere, turned all exposed skin red with burn, and pacing around awaiting one of each day's three big events – mealtime. And what a bad joke mealtime was. Each day's complete ration for three, packed in 12"x12" airtight plastic bags, meant never enough to go around. Each bag contained:*

> - *1 pack drink mix (Gookinade or Koolaid)*

- *2 packs granola with freeze dried blueberries or raisins (Mountain House)*
- *1 large bar chocolate*
- *1 pack compressed bacon bar or freeze dried sausage sticks (Mountain House)*
- *3 packs Mountain House fruit and nut trail mix*
- *2 packs Mountain House main course (lasagna, chop suey, beef stew, etc.)*
- *2 packs freeze dried strawberries or peaches*
- *3 packs of instant soup*

The plan was simple: breakfast was three spoons of the granola then pass the bag around the circle until both bags were empty, add one third of a bacon bar or sausage and some tea and it was all gone before you even had time to enjoy it. Split a chocolate bar and a pack each of trail mix – this was lunch. The rule was hard and fast: three spoons and pass on breakfast, five and pass on supper, and two and pass on dessert. Every fifth day's ration pack was a bonus pack and included a whole chocolate bar for each of us! Come on, day five!

The ration situation, small as it was, left us each feeling as though we were slowly starving to death. To make matters worse, I imagined that Hugh (who I was already feeling some animosity towards) was getting more on each spoonful than Mike or (more importantly) myself. I kept my feelings about this "total injustice" to myself but inside, the fire was well established. Fortunately, at this stage of the game we were still supplemented by fresh food we had purchased in Mendoza. To further aggravate the situation, water was becoming an increasing nuisance to obtain as when the temperature was cold, the tiny trickle of water from the hills to our east completely subsided, rendering us dependent on whatever snow happened to fall. On at least one occasion we spent the entire day scraping with our cups the one quarter of an inch of snow off the dirt to melt for the day's water requirements. The base camp was getting to be a bigger piss off by the day. Finally, day eight arrived and with it something that 'had' to be done (hallelujah!) – a round trip walk to Confluencia to drop off supplies. Any survivors of this forthcoming epic would have to pass Confluencia either in retreat from Plaza Francia and the South Wall, or the glorious victors of the mountain descending by normal route and the Plaza de Mulas. Left at this cache was some food, a few extra clothes from base camp and a few odds and ends, to include our Bo Derek edition of Playboy, the single most valuable base camp accessory. We ceremoniously waved our good-byes to Bo as we closed the bag and stashed it under some rocks on the Plaza de Mulas side of the

Horcones River. Optimism abounds. A pleasant walk back up the trail, gratified in the knowledge that something productive had finally taken place. From now on our lives would be a programmed response to two years of planning. Next agenda item – moving just the base camp to the foot of the mountain, poised for the start. Our actual technical equipment, ropes and other paraphernalia, we had conveniently hung at the start of the route by the use of a few ice screws. Day ten was for complete rest and fattening up on all the extra food that we had ratholed in case of weather delays in the base camp. We feasted on extra chocolate, dried meat and the last of the fresh fruit. And then, as if part of some ordered scheme, the hour slips to midnight, the skies parted exposing the full moon and it was Leap Year's Day, February 29, 1980.

Top: Author, at right, with Hugh at Base Camp, Plaza Francia (photo by Brian Berg). Bottom: Brian and the author contemplating the Face at Base Camp (photo by Hugh Grandfield).

Top: Today you would say "selfie." From left to right are Brian, the author and Hugh at Base Camp. Bottom: The climbers' lone tent at Base Camp, giving an idea of the isolation experienced at the time.

Base Camp, Plaza Francia

Top: View of the start of the avalanche from Base Camp. The Face is over two miles distant. Bottom: The avalanche track is about a half mile wide.

Top: The full scale of the avalanche is difficult to capture in photos. Bottom: Route as climbed by the author, with the lower variant (in yellow), then joining the French Route and finishing with the Messner exit.

Base Camp, Plaza Francia

The author with his "borrowed" boots at Base Camp (photo by Brian Berg).

5

Final Approach Trek

On February 29, 1980, we set off from base camp carrying everything but our climbing gear, which we'd previously pegged to the left-hand side of the base of the central pillar.

It was mostly overcast, not super-hot, but I was already laboring and sweating under a significant load and was not looking forward to the additional weight of the climbing gear – and then to actually climb a technical route requiring balance, strength and delicate moves.

We had hiked to the bottom of the Face and to our chosen destination at least once, but that was with day packs and lots of energy. Now, carrying a nearly full load, straining to lift our chins and look up at the vertical wall in front of us, the reality of climbing high-angle rock, vertical chimneys, and ice with a 50-plus pound pack began to sink in.

We snaked along the side of the moraine (also called glacial till – a mass of sediment and rocks carried down by a glacier), at its edge, sometimes on and sometimes off a faint trail left by previous climbers or trekkers going to the base of the Face itself. Progress was slow but steady as the path was walkable at times, and often not, with small ankle breaking crevices and holes. Brian and I ranged on ahead, leaving Hugh to get some camera shots of the stupendous views and magnificent terrain. Brian and I were not quite in the individual 'zen' like mindset of simply placing one foot in front of the other, but close.

We carried on a loose conversation, punctuated by curses as one or the other of us nearly fell prey to a hole or crevice. We debated as to whether it might give us faster progress to move left and travel uphill closer to the center of the moraine and former floor of the glacier. We had walked previously in that area on conditioning hikes and had noted the surface was filled with patches of pretty soft snow, wet in places and without consistent footing. We decided to stay on the side of the moraine.

After probably 45 minutes of hiking, we were adjacent to the mouth of a mini canyon descending from the ridge line to our right. Suddenly, without warning, there was an immense, grinding, freight train-like noise that filled the air, surrounding us, vibrating up into the soles of our feet. Not thinking, and incapable of being heard if we had tried to speak, we both dove to our right toward a two-to three-foot-high lip at the edge of the moraine itself. After what seemed like an eternity, but was probably about one second, a rock, ice, snow and boulder avalanche swept directly over our tiny refuge. We watched in fascination, trepidation and detachment as the mass of debris roared and flowed overhead, between 30 feet and as close as three feet above us. There was dirt, chunks of ice, VW-size boulders and lots of snow. The air was full of dust, snow, particles of rock, whatever. If our tiny earthen embankment had given way, or if there was enough debris to completely fill the area around us, there would have been little we could have done – we would simply have been entombed. Within 30 seconds, silence once again reigned, and we could hear Hugh shouting and screaming from some 200 yards downhill, hoping we were still alive, and not buried. We popped up to our feet, waving and shouting back.

And without further ado, Brian and I then moved posthaste toward the center of the moraine, away from the edges.

Welcome to the climb, I thought.

As we continued trekking up the moraine and another hour passed, we got to within 300 yards of the foot of the Face itself and were reminded that we should put on our climbing helmets by the whizz-thud sounds of falling rocks coming down at great speed from the heights above.

Oh, yes, we didn't **have** our helmets, as they were hanging with our climbing gear on a rock slab beside our starting point for the climb. We had left them with our gear on our final recce and conditioning hike to the bottom of the Face when the weather was about 20 degrees cooler... with no rock fall.

The impact zone was from about 50 meters to 250 meters out from the base of the Face. Okay, we thought, we'll pick those up early tomorrow when it's colder as we start up the route itself. So, we moved across the moraine away from the foot of the Face to our selected advance base camp area and set up for the night.

The conversations that evening were somewhat mixed, centered around our meager meals, the weather and the state of the mountain in as much as we had been hearing or seeing an avalanche nearly every day – and today, Brian and I had narrowly escaped being buried or struck by one. We had high hopes that most of the heavy accumulations of new snow were behind us, though why we thought that way I'm not sure. We reviewed who was going to carry what in the morning, and the best way to break things out or divvy them up so that our loads would be more or less equal. We could see that our original idea to have one pack a little lighter so that person could lead was not going to be possible. We would undoubtably be changing rope leads during the day, moving from one section to another and perhaps even on the same section.

I was a little apprehensive about Brian and Hugh's tendency to try and get a few more minutes of rest in the morning and not getting going early. A bit of a delay in starting the day could mean missing a valuable hour of stable snow. The bickering between Brian and Hugh waxed and waned. I did not like being in the middle, but there was no way I was going to take sides. I just hoped it wouldn't become demoralizing for any one of us. One by one, we drifted off to sleep.

The South Face: Central pillar and rib defining the route (photo by Hugh Grandfield).

6

Gaining the Central Pillar

U pon reaching our gear cache the next morning, we divvied up the equipment, adjusted gear and donned our packs again. *Holy shit,* I thought, *how am I ever going to climb with this pack on?*

We set about negotiating the very first pitch. To gain access to our route proper, we needed to scramble up, over and through snow and some loose rock to the left-hand side of a large, striated rock promontory that defines the bottom of the Face into a left- and right-hand side. About 2,000 vertical feet high, the promontory lies at the foot of a partial rib descending from about one-third to halfway up the face. I believed from earlier study of long-distance photos and looking at the rib that it would provide some degree of safety from avalanche and falling rock. Everything falling from high up should go to one side or the other on its way down. Once on the top of this huge rock outcropping, we would gain the rib and follow it directly up to the Broken Towers. Transitioning from the angled snow ramp to the side of the gigantic promontory and onto the rib itself would become technical but looked doable. We would be on this rib for the first part of our ascent.

As we set foot on the snow ramp beside this mammoth block, we instantly began cursing the loose, soft snow that swallowed your leg to thigh and crotch depth. Forcing a trail uphill was slow – really, really slow, and none of us wanted to lead. (*Who would be stupid enough to actually want to lead through that?*)

I suppose we each took turns slogging out a path for the others, but I am also sure we each felt someone else could have done more and taken up the lead longer. I know I did. Picture yourself trying to walk through five-foot deep, semi-soft snow, where each time you took a step and placed your boot onto the snow it sank easily at first. And then, compacting the snow beneath, coming to a rest about knee deep. Then as you put your weight on your leg, your boot punched through to where the snow level was about to your crotch or waist deep. Only then could you forcefully lift your other leg from the snow, lifting and attempting to drag it forward for the next plunging step. Now picture this with a 50-pound pack on. Now picture this on a 40 to 45 degree slope at 13,500 feet above sea level. Ahhh, the joys of "climbing."

The snow ramp gave way to rock and the ascent actually became enjoyable for a while. As the rock became steeper, we were faced with a bit of fifth-class climbing and roped up but were finally making progress without the enormous effort through the snow.

A segue for the reader who may not be familiar with climbing ratings or grade:

There are many numbering or grading systems in place. Different areas of the world and different countries have developed their own. Some systems are used only for rock, or complex bouldering problems, big mountains or ice. Other systems incorporate a number or letter for the length of the climb either in time it takes to complete by a 'normal' climber, or a combination of distance and altitude gained. Many multi-day routes on challenging peaks might include three or four ratings, each pertaining to certain aspects of the mountain. In this context, I loosely use a scrambling system based on the Yosemite Decimal System (YDS) which was originally developed by the Sierra Club in the 1930s. In the YDS, the specific numbering scale to grade routes on high angle rock was added in the 1950s by experienced Southern California climbers. It was at first, primarily based on routes found on Tahquitz Rock in Idyllwild, California (where I learned to climb) and quickly spread to the rest of the Americas. In the YDS, basic routes on high angle rock begin at 5.0 and continue on with 5.1, 5.2, etc. In the original concept, the grading ended at 5.9 with grade 6 representing the beginning of aid climbing. Before long, climbers had pushed the envelope and rock climbs of harder than 5.9 had been done, so the addition of two digits after the 5 came into use (5.10, 5.11, etc.).

Another climbing scale in use in many areas of the world was developed by the International Climbing and Mountaineering Federation which is known by the initials of its proper name in French, the UIAA. Suffice it to say that the grading of routes and climbing moves is complex, especially on big mountains where weather or different amounts of snow and ice will change the difficulty from year to year or even within the same season.

To adequately describe the difficulty of a route on a big mountain usually requires more than one grade, such as, rock difficulty, aid climbing difficulty, ice climbing difficulty, mixed climbing difficulty, steepness, length, level of commitment and others. For anyone interested in further reading on the subject, there is an excellent Wikipedia article on the grading of climbing routes that summarizes various systems in use (en.wikipedia.org/wiki/Grade_(climbing)).

As an aside, The French Route with the Messner exit comprises many different rock, snow and ice sections and today these have been generally graded with some at YDS 5.4 and others at 5.9. The UIAA grade is III to VI. However, to my knowledge, in 1980, there had been no grading assigned, and there certainly was no detailed guidebook.

We simply went and climbed.

In my usage here, Class One climbing is really no climbing at all, but a hike, with no hands required for balance. Class Two may occasionally require some hands on for balance, not too much exposure, and a fall will hurt but usually not injure you. Class Three often requires hands on for balance, some moves may be somewhat difficult, and a fall will usually result in breaking a bone. Class Four requires hands on most of the time, moves are often complex, with exposure such that a fall may result in death. Novice climbers may rope up at this level, and even experienced climbers might use a rope on a fourth-class portion in bad visibility, high winds or near incapacitation. And Class Five is technical rock climbing and almost everyone uses a rope at this point. Exposure may be tens to thousands of feet. A fall without protection will almost always be fatal.

We eventually gained the top of the gigantic rock promontory and pushed upward. Now truly on the rib, we found it became well-defined, with a large, wide couloir falling off to the right side (looking at the Face). To the other side, on our left and lower down, was our snow, ice and rock ramp. Looking toward the valley below, there was perhaps 55 yards of broken rib before it dropped off vertically, forming the face of the gigantic promontory.

Far above was a near vertical rock band we knew as the Broken Towers, sometimes referred to as the Great Towers. This rock band has a bulge in the center causing each side to angle off slightly. That bulge forms a division in the fall line and provides a little protection on it and directly below it as things falling from above – rocks, snow and ice – will mostly fall to one side or the other, and not straight down. Looking around our immediate area, we saw a small, almost level area of dirt. This is where we decided to pitch our tent.

The setting was spectacular. We had a space of some seven by eight feet on dirt and rock. Once the tent was pitched, the rib with its boulders and rocks were on three sides. The fourth side of the tent was about a foot from the edge of the rib where it dropped into the big couloir off to the right. There, if you were to stretch out your arm and drop a coin it would fall about 2,000 feet before hitting anything. To the other side of the tent and below was the snow and rock ramp we had ascended.

Above us were the Broken Towers, with seemingly never ending, impressive, vertical chimneys or fissures in the rock. Impossible in length, but to be our next stage. This major section of rock would be one of the deciding points in our attempt. In front of us, the lesser Horcones River Valley and the approach to the Face were laid out in grandeur. The view was magnificent and humbling.

We still had a couple of hours of daylight and while Brian was finishing the tent and organizing our gear, Hugh and I did a recce of the route ahead.

Our progress was really slow again as fresh snow from the night before still covered much of the rock uphill. This part was initially fourth-class scrambling – by braille. You could not see the rock underneath with its holes, angles and crevices. After a while, though, it was clear we should have unimpeded access to the base of the Broken Towers.

On that recce we did not, however, find another place for a decent tent site which meant that when we departed our current camp, we might need to make the top of the Towers in one long push. Upon our return to the now erected tent, it began to snow again heavily.

The next morning it was still snowing lightly with the cloud base just above us. With the snowfall of the night before, we were concerned about stuff (as in an avalanche) coming down from the Towers themselves, so were not too keen on getting very close to their base. We decided to wait and see what the weather would do, and all agreed that we would definitely stay the night where we were. We remained tent bound as the snow continued.

Later that afternoon, we heard a rushing noise, soft at first, then a bit louder, then of truly epic proportions. An avalanche was cascading down the couloir beside us, 50 yards away. The tent fluttered from the wind generated by the pressure wave from the avalanche. We had spindrift and boiling powder snow from above and from the side, which lightly covered the tent, but other than that, we were sound.

It was, all in all, a good place to be.

Day rolls into night, there was more bickering between Brian and Hugh, and I was feeling like a referee. I had to sleep between them, literally. Talk was about many things but always returned to food. The next day we looked at the rib which now had several feet of new snow. We realized we were not going anywhere soon.

This is just not good, I thought. We were now hoping that when the weather did clear, the snow would ablate away, quickly exposing the rib once again. The clouds lifted a little and Hugh and I decided to continue the recce we had started the earlier day and explore as close to the base of the Towers as we dared. It was more of the same, though this time, we did find an acceptable tent site.

The closer to the rock band we got, the more intimidating and challenging the section became. Some 1,000 to 1,100 feet high, this band is split by numerous fissures forming near vertical chimneys that looked to be between 500 and 600 feet in height. Looking up, from the base of the band, we knew immediately we weren't going to be able to finish it that same day. We're thinking that with luck, another day in relative protection might give the mountain time to settle and not shrug off more snow in yet another massive avalanche.

Back at the tent, Brian was grumpy, and I was hoping it was just from being in the tent all day. It was snowing lightly again and continued into the next day. I was beginning to worry about our slow progress. We had already used up all of our "delay" days and a couple more. I'm sure Brian and Hugh must have been thinking the same, but no one said anything about bailing. We stayed mostly in the tent, not wanting to be outside and leaving what we thought to be the safest spot within several hundred meters. *This is for the shit*, I thought. We came to the realization that we were going to have to push through it or bail.

Brian describes our first several days on the rib:

"... As the other two scouted the skyward front on this battle zone, I set to the task of cutting the platform and erecting the tent. The site was perfect, right on a protected rib of the ridge with a perfect view of the snake-like Horcones Glacier. The other two explorers soon returned, no big horror stories, just hard but straightforward climbing, came their report.

The weather unfortunately was not destined to be as straightforward. By mid-afternoon it was snowing with determination. An avalanche of unbelievable size swept the face to our right sending wind driven snow to nearly cover our tent. The snow and storm continued throughout the night. One day of vertical achievement and already locked in combat with this wicked wretch. To move camp forward the following day was out of the question. The snow, now thigh deep and still falling, made a mockery of any aspirations of forward progress and we were forced to stay in the same bivy for several days. Not part of the plan.

Broken Towers: Chimneys of 1,000 feet of vertical (photo by Ed Connor).

7

The First Rock Band
The Broken Towers

O nce deciding we needed to push on instead of retreating, we packed everything and finally moved slowly up the rib, trying our best to avoid the ankle breaker holes. The rib was now flattening, almost non-distinct as we got closer to the base of the first rock band. There was a section of broken rock to our right with easy access to the couloir that had so far channeled all falling snow, ice and rocks. A little above that we needed to ascend a short section of 80- to 90-degree angle rock. As I was leading out, I discovered older (really old) remains of ropes and pitons. We suddenly realized we were now directly on the original route done by the French in 1954! A humbling and inspiring moment.

Not too far beyond that was the base of the first large rock band. How I wished that I had no pack and no load to further complicate the moves that I was making. I found myself in awe of the French team that so many years before us had labored up the same exact spot, not knowing if they were going to be able to push onward or not. There came a spot where I could see what I needed to do but decided it was just too damn difficult with 45 pounds on my back and resorted to placing a pin and standing in stirrups. Hugh or Brian would remove it as they came up later. Often, in an alpine ascent with a pack on, in order to move forward and not become stalled, one may resort to direct aid. I did exactly that in a couple of cases along the route, but it is a trade off as you have to take the time to adequately place your anchor, clip in, transfer weight, re-position, etc. For anchors or protection on rock we carried no bolts, but a small selection of pitons (iron and titanium) and some assorted nuts and chocks.

Brian's journal notes:

> Forward progress was ours again on the following morning. Past more fixed ropes and hardware (left by previous teams), some very old, we made our way upward through the rocks to a short, very pleasant ice ramp and around a nasty exposed corner guarding another long ice ramp. This ramp, covered with deep snow, was very exposed, unprotected and fortunately easy. Tension erupts into temper when Hugh rejects my slightly authoritarian leadership. My displeasure is centered around his failure to remain on the safety line at all times.
>
> Our loads were not allowing us to streak up this so far moderate climbing, but we were secure in the

knowledge that we had no "extras." Still we could easily have managed as much vertical rise in one day (as it had taken us so far) if unencumbered by these loads. All the way to the Broken Towers this day, pegging the rock gear in place. Then a retreat for me to prepare another platform for our tent while Mike leads out on the first pitch of the 1,000-foot high towers on direct aid. The conquest of the Broken Towers will signal the no retreat mode of this climb.

A short segue:

Brian and I did not just come from a rescue background, it defined part of our psyche. On rescues and most high angle work, we were used to secondary or even tertiary anchors. Clipping into an anchor or rope was ingrained. It was a habit.

There are some downsides to being roped together, however. For instance, if one person on a rope falls on a steep snow slope while others are walking, that person can pull everyone else off. And, when lead climbing, especially at certain moments, on certain pitches, the rope drag itself or the movement caused by straining to bring up the rope attached to you, places one more at risk of falling than an individual climbing move without being clipped in.

But, almost always, being clipped in on a multi-person climb adds safety. On glacier travel, if one person falls into a crevasse the other has the opportunity to arrest their partner's fall. If a lead climber has a belay and falls – for whatever reason, the belayer can usually stop their partner's fall. We had this hammered into us during training.

So, we clipped in.

Hugh just didn't see the need to clip in when he felt he was in a secure position on the mountain.

When we finally set off up into the towers it was quite interesting, really. This immense rock band is striated with vertical grooves or cracks. These fissures, or wide cracks in the rock, form classic, rather long chimneys. So, if you like to stem, you would be in heaven. There were sections of about 300 to 500 vertical feet of chimney without so much as a bend.

If you are not familiar with stemming, it is a climbing technique in which the hands and/or feet are pressured in opposition far out to each side. Imagine a door frame or narrow corridor and putting your feet and hands on opposite sides and using counter-pressure to hold in place and move upward like a worm. It is not terribly difficult and is a relatively easy technique to master but does require some strength.

Picture yourself in a U-shaped crack in the rock with the back wall at about an 80-degree vertical angle, and the side walls between three and five feet apart. Now picture yourself 300 feet up the chimney with another three or four hundred vertical feet to go – with a fully loaded pack.

Focus. Fun.

Once again, we saw proof that we were directly on the French Route. We could see old pitons and sections of massive ropes, sometimes exposed, sometimes buried in ice. All of it deep within the very chimney we had selected to climb. It was fascinating and I was again feeling emotional. As I was hammering in yet another piton for protection that Hugh or Brian would remove on their way up, it occurred to me that I could probably use some of the French hardware still embedded in the rock to save time. So I did.

After hours of worming slowly upward, I began to hate the 40 plus pounds in my rucksack – like, really-tired, leg-cramping, arm- and wrist-trembling, shoulders-complaining hate. Even though I was resting at the end of each rope length, suspended by an anchor every 75 to 100 feet or so while I belayed Hugh up to me, I kept my pack on as it was too much trouble and effort to take it off, clip it to the anchor, bring Hugh up, put the pack back on, get everything unclipped, etc. Eventually, Brian began his ascent of the chimney, making pretty decent time as he was using a rope from Hugh's position as a safety line with an ascender on it. He could go at his own pace. On his way up Brian was finishing the cleaning process, making sure all our pins were removed in order to use them again if need be.

Nearing the end of the Towers, and thoroughly tired and grumpy, I finally decided that I would finish the lead without my ruck. I would put it on a rope and climb and then haul it up to me. I told Hugh the plan and once more brought him up to me.

With my pack secured to the rock, and without its weight and bulk, I could actually move! At the exit of the towers, I found a good belay position, rigged a mechanical advantage (a 2:1, Z-pulley system) and I hauled the damn pack up to me. There was a lot of friction, and that, combined with the normal stretch in the rope, made for a slow, laborious haul. In the Z-pulley system (sometimes referred to as the Yosemite hauling system), you typically use your legs to push a loop on a line attached to an ascender which pulls on the hauling line. Your legs are stronger and last longer than your arms.

After the very energy-sapping leg exercise of bringing my pack up, I then, of course, had to belay Hugh and Brian up. That involved no end of effort because it wasn't just them, but I had to help take up the weight of their packs as well.

That evening we finally made the top of the Broken Towers and gained the first, or inferior glacier. We had an uneventful night on the snow field of the glacier. In retrospect, it was very exposed avalanche-wise.

But we were lucky.

I think that night that we all realized just how short we were on food. We were now openly staring at one another as we were eating…

Remember the whole 'two-person meal serving three people' thing in order to save weight? Well, to recap, the re-hydrated meals were in bags and because we didn't have individual plates or bowls in order to save weight, we needed to pass them between us. So, as we passed around our dinner meal in its jumbo plastic bags, we decided the best way to share equally was literally by taking only three mouthfuls at a time. Each of us, in turn, would take three spoonfuls and then pass on the bag.

Of course, we were now carefully watching to make sure that not only were there just three spoonfuls, but that they were all the same size. We even made sure the spoons held the same amount…

We all knew at that point we were going to be somewhat hungry by the time we finished the climb. I did a rough calculation about the food. If I was right, we had consumed over a third of our food supply but were less than a third of the way up the Face. And, by the way, that would be a third of our **total** food supply, including the reserves.

That was the night I also noticed some of stitching on the welts of my borrowed Triplex boots starting to disintegrate. This was allowing the layers of the sole to begin to separate and come apart. The glue that had been helping to attach the sole onto the plastic stiffener plate had long ago disintegrated. Combined, that had the potential to be rather serious as the very bottom of the boot, the Vibram sole, was attached to the upper boot only by this thread.

If it continued to disintegrate, the Vibram sole would separate completely from the boot, flapping. *Well, I thought, things were now becoming truly interesting. Okay, I'll take some paracord and encircle the boot, pressing the cord into the spaces between the ribs and lugs on the sole and tie it off on top. That should hold the sole on while I was using the boot on rock.* And then I rationalized that as long as I had my crampons laced onto my boots, I didn't really need the stitching. With the crampon fixed onto the bottom of the sole and laced tightly to the upper boot, the sole wasn't going to move. As it turned out, the paracord worked after a fashion, but when on rock, without the crampon on, it abraded so quickly I needed to change it every day. And, because we didn't have an unlimited supply, eventually I ran out. I'm not sure why I didn't realize then that there were other issues with the boots as well. Nor did I think as to what would happen when I didn't need, or couldn't use the crampons, like on descent and on the trek back to civilization.

As we settled in for the night, there was less bickering between Brian and Hugh for once. We were all pleased we had moved beyond the Great Towers. We regarded them as one of the major difficulties of the route. (We would find out in a couple of days that the mountain had many more difficulties in store for us.) We knew that the morrow would bring us to the Sandstone Band and we expected to finish that and move up the second glacier to the start of the Messner variant by tomorrow evening.

I think we were all concerned about our food supply and the fact we were constantly hungry, certainly losing weight at this point.

I had my own issues going on with the disintegration of my boots and was hoping they would last through the climb and descent. We ended up sleeping pretty well that night, with no snow, no wind nor any avalanche seen or heard.

Top: Close-up of the ice nose on the second rock band. Bottom: Second rock band -- our route is on the left hand side of the image (photos by Ed Connor).

8

Sandstone Rock Band
Leader Fall

From the lower glacier we moved up to the base of the second rock band, which we knew as the Sandstone Band. Supposedly, this section offered moderate climbing and from photos and a distance below, looked like it would be all rock. A section of the same surface would be much easier than mixed snow, then ice, then rock, then ice, etc. We needed to finally make some real progress upward as we were way behind on food, energy and morale – being delayed by so many days of bad weather and incredible snow had taken its toll.

As we started up the second rock band, I thought, *this was going to go well, and fairly quickly*. It didn't. The angle was not too bad, at least at first, and from where we were, it looked to be only 500-600 feet high. Just at the top of the band was a section of ice seracs at the edge of the glacier above it. (This was the glacier with a three-quarter mile wide, 50 to 200 feet high terminus that had calved off and dropped 1,000 feet onto the glacier below in the epic avalanche we had witnessed in base camp.) The vertical face of the serac directly above us was kind of like a nose or a prow, and once you were at its base, was only about 15-20 feet high. It, too, looked pretty doable from below.

We moved up the rock band delicately but relatively easily at first, actually making decent progress. Just as the angle increased, we came to a small bench, or rock ledge, about a foot wide. It was perfect for lunch and to set up a belay. Looking up, I wondered where the best line would be. It was beginning to look complicated with many patches of verglas on top of the rock. The good thing, from our mini lunch spot, it looked like we could finish the rock band in one long pitch. Then, where the angle eased, we could transition a few more feet right up to the base of the serac.

I ended up leading again with Hugh belaying me. In short order, I found that next part of the rock band was worrisome. The rock above me was indeed now mostly covered by a quarter of an inch to six inches of ice, so it was back to climbing with crampons on. The angle was too steep to step sideways, angulating your ankle, and I needed to front point. The going was super delicate. I could usually get enough penetration with my axe and hammer (as long as I didn't over-swing it) and gingerly continued upwards. Occasionally, when the ice was thin, the point of the axe or hammer would pull or bounce out, bringing small chunks of ice with it. I tried several times to place an ice screw for protection but got no more than about an inch of penetration with the screw before the ice around it fractured and simply popped out in dinner-plate size. To make things worse, for the most part, you couldn't make out the detail of the rock beneath the verglas. So, seeing a crack or crevice in the rock underneath the ice, and then clearing the ice on top of it in order to hammer in a pin or place one of our few chocks or nuts wasn't possible either. I was about 10-20 feet above Hugh with no protection in place and realized that this section was not going well. In fact, it was going poorly. I kept looking for a place to put in a screw or hammer in a pin – but could not find anything. I was beginning to sweat mentally and tried to slow my breathing.

Hmmm, I thought, *okay, it looks like I can put something in just a little farther*. And so it went, until I realized I was about 50 feet out, still with no protection between Hugh and me. I was now looking at the possibility of a 50-foot fall to Hugh's position and then 50 feet more before coming to tension on the rope. I was pretty nervous at this point and was having trouble staying focused. I suggested to Brian he look at an alternate line to the right of where I was.

Brian started up. It did not look like he was going to be able to drop a rope to me anytime soon for belay, but he found easier ground and at least he was moving. I did not feel comfortable staying motionless and needed to move – up, down, or laterally. I made sure Hugh was well set and decided to continue. More of the same.

I was now about 80 feet out with no protection and trying to remain focused and not consider the possibilities, all of which were not good. I kept looking around and finally saw what I thought would give a decent combination for foot and ice tool placements. I let Hugh know I could see the angle ease and that there was a nice finish to this pitch about eight feet higher. And I told him I was going to see if it would go. He said he was ready.

I was balanced, both feet well placed with front points in and reaching up, I got a good bite with the hammer in my left hand. I delicately removed the axe in my right hand from the ice and reached up to swing it for the next purchase. I don't know if there was a gust of wind or my pack shifted due to the reach and start of my arm swing, but I suddenly found myself with a slight rotation to the left. If it continued, I would simply overbalance too far to the left and peel off the rock. I instinctively began to counter the rotation with a slight twist of the hammer in my left hand.

POCK!

The ice around the hammer popped away from the rock in a plate-sized chunk and I was now falling backwards, head over heels. This was going to be about a 160-foot leader fall.

Any fall is not good, and a leader fall especially so. Apart from hitting something at the bottom and the obvious fractures, if you are tumbling, there is also the risk of dislocating a joint and becoming incapacitated. Being severely injured or incapacitated is actually worse for your climbing partners than dying – for if you die, they can opt to leave you in place instead of somehow rescuing you. Also, in a fall, there is the probability of losing gear or equipment – thereby complicating your remaining climb if you are lucky enough to survive and recover. And, of course, if you are directly above your belayer, without sufficient protection in, you run the risk of hitting them on the way down, injuring them or worse, in the process.

I don't remember thinking the proverbial, *oh, shit!* but I do remember being really pissed and profoundly regretful that I was probably going to hit Hugh and to pull him off the ledge, ending up killing him in the process.

I cartwheeled down the face, bouncing with pretty good impacts on the rock, sometimes absorbed by my pack or helmet, sometimes not. I came to a stop mostly horizontal, face up, a bit head low, cheek against the rock. Hugh let me know he's still there by asking if I was still alive and if I could hear him. I could. He needed me to take my weight off the rope so he could regroup. After a quick assessment I found I could move all my parts, and nothing appeared broken. Even better, nothing appeared to be dislocated, and I still had my pack, strapped on tight. My neck and head seemed fine, and I had good grip strength in my hands. I had my ice hammer though I lost my axe in the fall. I slowly got rearranged and back on my feet and realized I was only about 30 feet below Hugh. He had seen me peel off the face and began taking in the rope as fast as he could as I was on my way down, so that when I passed him, he was able to begin an immediate braking process in a perfect and classically done belay. I had felt no real impact at the bottom of fall. Brian, looking at it all from the side, was in disbelief. He was sure at first that we were both gone, and then with Hugh still in place, he was sure that I was dead, or at least severely injured. I admitted to them that I didn't feel up to leading again beyond Hugh right away. Brian said no worries as he thought he had found an easy way to the base of the seracs above us.

I was thinking, *great, now he tells us...*

Brian managed to angle up and over to the base of the serac above and set up a belay, dropping a rope down. I was able to climb up to Hugh and our lunch spot on the bench that had served us so well. Hugh then got up to Brian assisted by being on belay while I rested. Together, Brian and Hugh helped me up to them. I found I could move without pain of any kind (other than a rather severe blow to my ego), and my physical condition and strength appeared to be the same as in the morning. We regrouped and moved slowly up another 100 to 300 feet to the base of the serac. We stood there looking up it, and although it was not too high at about 15-20 feet, it was absolutely vertical. The lip or transition from the vertical ice to the near horizontal surface of glacier above was going to be delicate and might require some kind of direct aid. Brian took us up and over the edge using his long arms to advantage.

9

The Second or Upper Glacier

With Brian on the glacier above belaying, it was now relatively simple for Hugh to move up the vertical ice of the serac and over the lip onto the glacier. Brian disappeared from view and Hugh, on the lip above, rested and organized the rope and his gear, and then it was my turn. The ice was wonderful in comparison to the thin, shitty stuff covering the rock band. It was, however, truly vertical so with a 50-pound pack on, your center of gravity or center of balance was behind you. Every move tended to pull you off backwards. I got over the lip and saw Brian in the distance, stomping out a platform in the snow for the tent. Hugh joined him while I was resting and organizing my stuff (both physical and mental). I was also trying to convince myself that I was not even a little bit shaken by my fall. I was having mixed success with that.

I wandered across the glacier following the two to three feet deep trail to where Brian and Hugh had the tent platform 90 percent stamped out. Where we were, from "front to back," the glacier was fairly short, maybe 200 yards or so. To put it another way, from the head of the glacier to the terminus or the downhill edge, was about 200 yards. From side to side, the glacier was wide for being on a steep face – three quarters of a mile or more. It was also where the original French Route traverses to the right across the glacier some 800 yards to three quarters of a mile before angling upwards again toward the summit ridge. As I was making my way slowly toward Brian and Hugh I was looking around and above.

Now composed again, I became aware of my surroundings and was beginning to 'feel' the mountain once more. I was becoming more and more nervous. I was feeling very, very exposed to anything coming down the face. Where we were was just so open to any rock, snow or ice sloughing off from above. Literally anything that came down from above would impact right where we were. By the time I reached the tent platform, now complete, I was convinced it was in a bad place and let the others know my thoughts. The retort was immediate – they were pissed and told me to "fuck off." They said they had worked hard on getting everything ready and reiterated this was where we were going to set up the tent. I tried to explain that I didn't think it was a good tent site. They were just not hearing what I was saying about a bad spot. The conversation became heated but got nowhere. We were all exhausted at that point. In retrospect I'm not too sure I was in the best frame of mind to articulate calmly why I thought the place wouldn't do. I ended up taking the tent from my pack – which, because I had been carrying it on that day, was the only reason they had not already finished setting it up – placed it on the snow and told them they could go ahead, but I was not staying there.

I began to force a path to a spot about 75-100 yards farther. It was not nearly so scenic and was mostly under a projecting large boulder. Brian and Hugh were in shock as I moved away. After about a minute, they picked up the tent and began to follow me. Cursing with every step, they let me know that we would go ahead and set up the tent where I indicate, but that I had better damn well stomp out the platform – they'd had enough.

How hard could stomping out a platform be? Well, you need to compact the snow until it will support your weight. Each step was into two- to three-feet deep snow before you could place all your weight onto your foot and not keep sinking. We needed a platform some seven by eight feet and could manage about ten by four inches of compacting for every two or three steps. Not hard at sea level but tiresome at 19,000 feet. After what seemed like an hour but was probably only a couple of minutes of solo work, Brian and Hugh began to help and, as daylight faded, we had a place to set up our abode.

We were all feeling a little better after our dinner (and of course, counting each other's spoonfuls and having made sure no one ate more than the other). Talk turned to progress and the remainder of the route. We felt we were now well and truly committed, and at this point it would be easier and safer to finish the climb rather than bail out and retreat. It was quite possible that with good weather we could make the summit, or at least the summit ridge, in one long push from where we were.

As I was getting ready to strip my outer layers and worm my way into my sleeping bag, I wiped my hands down my legs. My right hand came away moist and a little sticky. Strange.

I cleaned my hands and went through the motion again. Same result. *Hmmm, something must be going on with my right leg*, I thought, and decided to take a closer look. I found a slit in my lower right pant leg and realized I really did need to examine my legs. *Perhaps I didn't escape my fall without a scratch after all.* Taking off my outer pants and pulling up my thermal base layer, I discovered I had two wounds on my right lower leg. They were oozing serous fluid, but not bleeding. One was an incision, as if made by a scalpel, about three inches long. It had opened like a pair of butterfly wings and looked to be about an inch to an inch and a half deep, close and parallel to the tibia, about a quarter inch to a half inch toward the lateral aspect, or the outside of my leg. The second wound was uglier, but less deep. It was a laceration with a flap that had been undercut. The skin and subcutaneous tissue had been cut and then pulled and ripped back exposing an area about an inch by two inches to a depth of about three quarters of an inch. The flap was still attached along the entire lateral side of the wound.

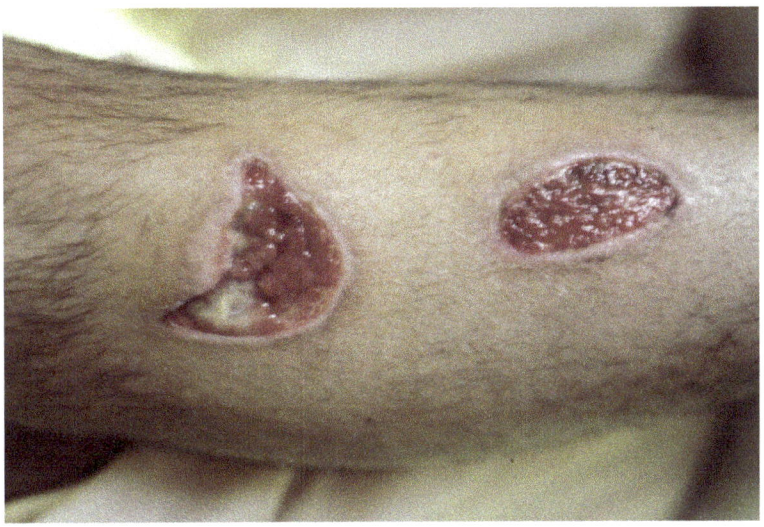

The author's right leg wounds -- about three to four weeks post-accident. Almost healed!

Brian and Hugh had not been paying attention until I exposed my lower leg. Hugh now looked sick, and Brian was instantly concerned, asking my thoughts. I did a self-assessment of the wounds, my condition, and our situation. I replied that the wounds needed to be cleaned and treated. I was going to need to begin an antibiotic regimen and might need help in wound management. Neither one was actively bleeding, and as best as I could tell, neither had hampered my movement in any way. They might have affected strength in the leg, but I didn't think so. Both wounds required closure, but that was not going to be possible given where we were. I would have to get by with cleaning and dressing them, and later, changing the dressing if possible. The flap we could simply clean and leave in place as it might help with healing.

After my wounds had been treated, Brian and Hugh were quiet and pensive. I sensed their question and told them that I thought I was good to go and was willing to continue the climb if they were. We all knew what was below us and we didn't want to retreat. From just outside the tent site we could see the finish. It seemed so close and most major difficulties seemed behind us.

The vote was onward and upward.

It was just daylight the next morning when we heard a rumble and a rushing sound. We now knew that sound intimately.

Shit!

The avalanche was loud and distinct...and **really** close. We zipped open the door of the tent and looked out from under the projecting boulder. There, 75 yards in front of us was a cascading 60-foot-wide column of snow and ice, impacting on the tent platform Brian and Hugh had prepared late yesterday afternoon. It lasted about 15-20 seconds and then all was quiet again.

Nobody said a word.

We decided to give the mountain another day to settle and spent yet one more day doing nothing. We were now down to one dinner meal and one complete meal packet (breakfast, lunch and dinner) with hopefully one day remaining to the summit. Then at least a day, maybe two, back to our cache at Confluencia.

However, we were acutely aware that with the atrocious weather we had experienced, we had consistently underestimated the delays we might encounter. The amount of fresh snow almost daily had severely hampered and slowed our progress. We were all concerned about any additional delays – they could put us seriously into a survival situation. We were already very hungry, and had been losing weight, strength and energy day by day.

That day and evening we consumed our next to last meal and prepared for what we hoped was to be our summit push on the morrow.

10

Off Route and Hanging Bivy

The next morning, we packed everything up and trudged the few remaining yards to the bergschrund which would be the start of the Messner variation, and with luck, our summit push. My right leg was feeling more or less okay, though stiff. The bandage was still clean on the outside. I didn't take it off or take a peek as we had limited first aid supplies. Other than a sore leg, I seemed to have the same number of places that normally hurt, so all in all it appeared that I came through the fall surprisingly well.

A bergschrund, or schrund, is a crevasse that forms at the head of a glacier, where the moving ice of the glacier separates from the headwall or ice on the rock above. It often extends down to bedrock so can be quite deep – dozens to hundreds of feet. A bergschrund is usually filled in with snow early in the climbing season, offering an easy (but requiring a careful) transition from the glacier to the ice or headwall above it. When not filled in, or only partially so, it can be a major obstacle in an otherwise accessible route or line on the mountain. The bergschrund that was confronting us was not very wide, perhaps about six feet and didn't appear to be too deep. There was soft snow on the other side. It was going to require a jump from the glacier to the headwall and a short climb on low angle snow.

The bergschrund on the upper glacier, with the Messner variant snaking directly up the middle of the image (photo by Ed Connor).

A segue here about some former training:

During pararescue training for glacier travel and snow and ice rescue, I had gone to Mt. Rainier in Washington, and along with 10-12 other young and not so young PJs, had learned the basics of boot-axe belays for your partner, self-arresting with an ice-axe if you slip or fall, and how that applies to a rope team of which you are part. We also practiced self-rescue from a crevasse, setting up a multi-point equalizing anchor system and hauling someone who was unconscious or injured out of the crevasse.

Of course, the only way to practice a self-arrest was to actually fall on a slope, begin sliding down and then arrest. After one try, it was so much fun we couldn't be stopped and tried to out-do each other. For the crevasse part, we had to rope up with a partner. We would simulate trekking not too far from the edge and then one of us would run and simply leap into the space of the open crevasse, trusting our partner to correctly and efficiently arrest our fall. Then, we would either ice climb the side of the crevasse or practice using a mechanical ascender (most of us had jumars).

Our instructor and mentor on the mountain, a senior PJ named Bob Watkins (whom we all revered), had to stop that exercise as we were soon trying to see who could leap the farthest into the crevasse.

So, I had no problem with a leap of faith – I decided I could give it a try and stomped out a path to the edge. I backed off and ran toward the crevasse, leaping toward the mountainside. I managed to make the other side but was unable to get any purchase in the soft snow on the other side with my hammer and gently fell back into the open space of the bergschrund. Brian had me on belay and, with assistance, I was able to easily climb (but with considerable physical effort) out of the crevasse and rejoin him and Hugh. While sort of simple, the landing in the snow and then half climbing and being half pulled back up the side of the crevasse was a lot of work. It was also a major pain in the butt, as snow was everywhere, up my sleeves, in my parka and down my neck. To top it off, it was melting, wetting all my top layers – and I was sweating my gonads off. Next it was Hugh's turn, and he chose a slightly different spot, then did a mirror performance to mine. Brian pulled him out. It was then Hugh's turn to curse and Brian's turn to try and cross. Brian chose yet a different spot. It was either a better place or maybe just that he had longer arms and legs, but he managed to gain the other side.

Now that Brian was across the bergschrund, he was able to bring Hugh across. Hugh, after his last effort and not super comfortable on snow and ice, wanted the belay from both sides, so went second. I followed and we were now ready to continue up the route. We got organized and looked up trying to judge the route above. There was a short, steep snow and ice ramp, then some nasty looking exposed rock, and then more snow and ice, and finally onto the upper snow and ice expanse to the summit ridge and col. We all got up to just below the exposed rock section and conferred, trying to judge the line and determine our climbing sequence.

I guess I was feeling grumpy, or perhaps I was feeling some soreness from the impacts against the rock during my cartwheeling 100 plus feet fall the day before. Whatever it was, I was definitely feeling like I didn't relish leading again right then. I told Brian that if Hugh really was the rock wizard Brian told me he was, then he needed to step up and lead. Brian, most certainly more diplomatic than I at that point, got Hugh to lead. And he did a superb job. Much, much better than I could have done, I thought. Hugh brought Brian up to him. They talked for a bit, then told me Brian was going to go on for another short pitch, bring Hugh up, and they would then bring me up. As Brian started climbing, I thought he might be angling too far to the left but couldn't really tell from my vantage point and didn't say anything.

When they were finally ready, I realized I had now been standing in one spot for what seemed like a couple of hours. My right leg was throbbing, and the wet upper layers of clothing from the attempt on the schrund along with the lack of movement and effort for over an hour had left me cold to the core. As I began to climb, I felt suddenly weak and had to tell Brian and Hugh I needed tension on the rope – lots of tension. They hauled me up and we ate our meager, last remaining lunch. Looking up, the view of the mountain was tremendously foreshortened, but we could actually see what appeared to be the route upwards and all the way to the col between the two summits and the Guanaco Ridge. If we could gain the snowfield today, we would be on the summit ridge by nightfall.

Brian led out and continued upwards until the angle increased to about 60 degrees or slightly more, then brought Hugh up. Now it was my turn, finally, and they belayed me up to them. The small amount of movement and the effort in that short pitch helped me warm up a little and to feel more human. We paused and conferred again. Brian and Hugh would continue to push the route and I would remain in place and belay them from where we were if I needed to. All around the area I'm standing on I was seeing signs of rock underneath the ice covering. The ice was thin, but it was thicker than the stuff we had encountered on the Sandstone Band. As they began to move upward, I looked around for a good spot to rest and belay from. I found a small, rounded bulge where the angle was about 30 degrees on top. That would suit me fine, though I wasn't able to sit down. Off to my immediate left was a steeper section of ice which appeared to be about six inches thick. After an hour or so, there had not been a lot of upward progress but there had been a lot of cursing. Looking up toward their position it appeared they had taken some easy ice angling off to the left and it had gotten steeper, and then directly above them was a 200 feet high, slightly overhanging rock and ice eyebrow. That was definitely not in the plan, nor on the route. I realized Brian and Hugh were not going to push the route onto the final snowfield from where they were and would most likely be returning to me.

Shit, I thought. If that happened, we would be screwed as it would mean we either had to move somewhere laterally, attempting to find the route at night with no working headlamps, or bivy on steep ice. There was nowhere to put a tent and no shelter unless we dropped back down about 400 vertical feet all the way to the delicate rock section that Hugh led us through. I was now looking for a spot to place an ice screw, or several, if I could. As I began the process, first one, then another attempt failed as the screw bottomed in about two inches of ice and popped out. After several more tries I got one really solid screw in the steep section of ice off to my left. However, the head of my eight-inch long screw with its attachment point was sticking out about three inches from the ice. I could not place it deeper without running the risk that it, too, would pop out. In order to avoid having to clip in at the head of the screw sticking out some three inches away from the ice, I took a runner and looped it around the screw where it penetrated the ice. That way I could avoid a moment arm of significant length that would weaken its holding power, and lever it out of the ice in the event of a fall.

Just after sunset, Brian and Hugh did, indeed, down climb to me and lost no time in asking where we were going to spend the night. I was somewhat taken aback by the directness of the question as there had been no discussion, no request to find a spot, even though I knew it was coming. I replied that there was no place to put a tent, and that we could possibly traverse and down climb. Or we possibly carve out a bench on the rounded bulge I'd been standing on. Brian looked around and asked about the screw... and said he would clip the tent in, and we could all crawl inside and hang, suspended, on the single screw. I mentally flashed back to the runners or slings from outside the tent sewn through the seam at the bottom to the inside that I thought we'd never use. I thought about the three of us inside the tent fighting for space – the tent had no rigid platform for the floor, and we didn't have a portaledge of any kind, so to be inside the tent suspended from one screw would be like being inside a large nylon bag or stuff sack suspended from a hook. I decided the screw was not going to hold all three of us wiggling and squirming around inside. I told him I wasn't going to use it, but they could, saying I felt that it might be okay for two, but not for three of us.

He went ahead and got the tent out, clipped in two points on the side of the tent to the screw, and motioned for me to go inside. I told him again I was convinced it would not hold the three of us all night. Brian and Hugh asked if I thought the screw was solid, and when I said, "yes," they responded, "well, if you say it's solid, we'll trust it." (Tests conducted 15-20 years or so after our climb show that a well-placed ice screw like we were using should give a holding power of about 7kN – 7 kilo Newtons – or roughly 1500 pounds.)

They crawled inside and while they were figuring out how to arrange themselves and the gear they took into the tent, I disconnected completely from all ropes and the screw. I made sure that if it did pull out, I was not going to be unceremoniously yanked off the side of the mountain in the mess of their fall. I managed to cut and chip out a small platform in the 30-degree ice surface of the bulge I was on. I now had a two by two-foot area to sit down on. It was not quite level, but close enough. I got a good placement with my ice hammer to the side of where I was perched and clipped in. If I did nod off in sleep or exhaustion the hammer would arrest my fall. I was now committed to sitting in place all night. I pulled out a small, closed-cell foam pad to sit on. Beginning years before in all my rucksacks I would custom fit a one quarter inch thick Ensolite (closed-cell foam) pad to go inside, next to my back. It served as padding from sharp or hard objects and could also be used as emergency insulation to sit on in a case like this. In over eight years of climbing, hiking and trekking, this was the second time I was going to use it. I figured out I could wrap my sleeping bag around my upper body. I still had my boots and crampons on, so I emptied my pack enough in order to stick my feet, boots on, crampons and all, inside it.

We were a little over 22,000 feet high at this point, and I was totally exposed, sitting on the near vertical face clipped into a hammer in the ice for protection. There were no low clouds, but a high haze somewhere around 30,000 feet, and best of all, no wind. As I began to settle in for what was to be a long night, I started to analyze my situation: We had been undernourished for the entire climb and all of us had lost weight, our bodies had used all our excess fat and were beginning to metabolize muscle mass. We had about a quart of water that entire day and were now suffering the effects of dehydration. At altitude the air is quite dry, and you lose up to twice as much or more water through insensible loss (unnoticed or unperceived loss) just through respiration. The very act of inhaling and then exhaling a breath transfers moisture from your lungs into the much drier air. In order to stay ahead of the dehydration curve, you need three or more quarts of water a day. Perched where I was, my legs were bent at the knee, and my crampons were still laced tightly to my boots, both of which were compromising circulation to my feet. Except for the episode with the bergschrund, I hadn't truly exerted myself all day and was still really cold. With a clear sky and no clouds, it was going to get much colder during the night, daytime air temps had been around minus 20 degrees Fahrenheit. At that point I became aware that I was not sure I could feel my feet or much of my lower legs and then I knew it was going to be one *really* long night. The realization slowly surfaced that I was going to suffer frostbite – severe frostbite. The question in my mind became, *how bad*?

As I was sitting there contemplating my navel, I began to look around, and even in the state I was in, I had to admit that the view was spectacular. I was looking at the surrounding hills and even though there was no moon yet, the peaks and ridgelines were distinct and faintly glistening, illuminated in the starlight. The bottoms of the twisting lowlands and the Horcones River Valley were lost in the darkness below. The stars near the horizon were bright, crystal clear and not twinkling, and I realized I was staring at the Southern Cross. Beautiful.

Throughout the night there was a lot of squirming and muttered curses from the tent...but the screw held.

11

Summit Snowfield Tragedy
Hugh Falls

The morning after the bivy was spectacularly beautiful. Not a cloud in the sky, visibility to forever, a slight breeze, and very cold. My hands and body were fine, but stiff. I couldn't feel my feet, so I didn't know how they are, but I assumed they were injured and frostbitten. I didn't know how much at this point.

It took what seemed like all morning for Brian and Hugh to get out of the tent and get organized. They let me know the route was not directly above us but must be off to the right. That was going to necessitate a horizontal traverse across 60 plus or minus-degree ice for about 200 yards. I ended up leading as I was closest, Hugh followed, and Brian brought up the rear. It was pleasant and terrifying at the same time. The ice was wonderful for a change – what I call "styrofoam" ice. It allowed for perfect front-pointing, absorbed any swing by your hammer or axe and gave superb holding. It was terrifying in that we were strung out on the traverse, with no protection at all, and Hugh, who was not confident on ice, in the middle. If anyone pulled off, we all would. After about 30 minutes, Brian remarked, "We're good. We can force the route from here." We moved straight up on ice that was gradually easing in angle and then in short order onto the summit snowfield. And at that moment we realized all difficulties were behind us. All we had to do was plod on and we would reach the col and then the summit.

As we got higher and the angle eased a little more, the ice turned to snow and then softened, and we were again plunge-stepping into two-feet deep snow, but at 22,500 feet. After a couple of hours Brian, who had been leading and creating a path for us, was absolutely fagged. He called for a change in leads. I had been trailing Brian with Hugh last in line. In order to change leads we needed to change position on the rope and began to do so. I unclipped from my knot but left the rope inside the carabiner and waited for Hugh to begin to pull the rope through from me to him. He would take my knot, clip in with mine, then unclip his knot at the end of the rope and toss it to me so I could clip into it. That way, if one of us were to slip, the others would still be able to arrest their fall. Hugh, for some reason – as he had done on many occasions during the climb – unclipped completely, hoping somehow to expedite the process, and tossed me the end of the rope. And I clipped in.

Suddenly, at that precise moment, the snow beneath him gave way slightly and he slipped and overbalanced. He fell backwards and Brian and I went immediately face down into an ice axe arrest position. My face was smashed in the soft snow, the pick of my hammer buried as deep as it would go, and I – while I was falling face flat – had positioned the hammer's shaft diagonally across and under my body to provide maximum weight and help prevent it from being jerked out of my hands if the rope went tight and pulled me. We were hoping against all odds that we could catch Hugh on belay if he could grab the rope.

I felt a slight tug on the rope and then nothing. When I looked up, Hugh was airborne, in the middle of a backflip, arms outstretched, mouth wide open and looking directly at me.

Many of the details of the climb are now fuzzy but that is one image that is still crystal clear in my mind.

There was nothing Brian and I could do except stare in horror and disbelief. Hugh continued to backflip down the snowfield we had just labored to climb, falling faster and faster, gaining tremendous speed. Coming to the upper edge of the 200-foot high, slightly overhanging ice eyebrow that had stymied our progress the day before, he was launched out into space, impacting on the glacier 300 feet below. He was still traveling at an incredible speed, cartwheeling, tumbling and flipping, and went for another 300 yards down the glacier toward its terminus before disappearing from our sight over the edge to impact several thousands of feet below.

We were shattered. There was absolutely no possibility he would have survived the fall.

I was shocked by the speed with which everything unfolded, my mind kept playing the scene in seeming slow motion. I was frustrated that I could do nothing to help and horrified that we had lost a friend. The realization that there was truly, literally, nothing we could do at that point did not make it any easier. I was staring down the summit snowfield and below it to the edge of the glacier below where Hugh had disappeared. Filled with frustration and resentment that I could do nothing, that there was no trick I could I somehow pull out of a magic bag that would change things, I kept repeating, *oh no, oh no*, over and over. Brian, undoubtably frustrated and thinking the same, said, "Come on, pull yourself together." I replied, "you're right," and we turned and continued upward.

It is one thing to mentally analyze a situation like this and determine there would be no chance of rescue or recovery, or in our case, of even descending to look for him. It is another thing entirely to *actually have* to put it aside and move on. We had no other choice. Any other option for us would have been fatal at that point in the climb.

Although near exhaustion, with Hugh's fall, Brian must have felt the need to work out his emotions and he continued to lead on... all the way to the col. It was more plunge-stepping, forcing a two-feet deep trail, but Brian didn't rest, even with my suggestions. Reaching the col, Brian plopped down, sitting, just over the crest of the Guanaco Ridge, motionless. He had a thousand-mile stare and mumbled that he couldn't help or do anything. It was now nearing sunset and with Brian not able or willing to move, I needed to get the tent up or find shelter.

With the onset of darkness, visibility was waning fast. Brian was practically incoherent, had no energy and was essentially non-responsive to any questions. I knew there were some shelter spots down the north side of the mountain but did not know exactly where. Taking time to adequately explore the area was a non-starter. My feet were still frozen from the night before. The idea of descending the Canaleta – the wide trough or somewhat open gully through which the climbing track from the north side ascended – and wandering around hoping to find something, then climbing back to Brian, then trying to escort him back down somewhere was just not possible for me. Nor was I going to leave him and set off on my own.

I decided to drop down a few feet on the north side of the Guanaco Ridge below its crest near the top of the Canaleta. There, the angle was only about 30-45 degrees, and I was able to cut and stomp out a level tent platform in the snow. Laboring with every breath from the altitude, I had to forcefully step into and stomp the snow in order to compact it and make the platform. As I was stomping and stepping into the snow, I was acutely aware of the condition of my feet and toes. The process didn't go quickly. I finally got the tent set up and used our three remaining ice tools (Brian's axe and hammer and my hammer) as anchors, passing the shafts diagonally through the tent tie down loops at the bottom edge of the tent, stomping on the head of each to well and truly bury it in the snow. It was all I could do to gather some large rocks and bury them as well for an additional anchor or two.

Brian was exhausted, remained immobile, nearly incoherent and still not answering any questions. With great difficulty, I got him inside the tent, took off his boots, partially undressed him and got him into his bag. It was now well after sunset, and I went about gathering some snow to try to melt for water as we hadn't had anything to drink for a day and a half and no food whatsoever for over two days. It was taking forever to melt the snow. I rummaged through both Brian's and my pack for the remaining meal I thought we had and realized it must have gone with Hugh. I managed to find one soup pack left in our gear and mixed that in with what water I was able make. I had just enough to fill each water bottle halfway. I ended up spoon-feeding Brian and forced myself to drink, nearly gagging in the process. I was exhausted, physically and mentally, drained by the thought of losing Hugh. There was an emptiness and a void, but no coherent thoughts.

A segue:

In my first draft, many of my personal emotions noted throughout were not expressed, however, Leah and Karesse, the two people who have helped guide me the most through this recounting with feedback and editing, and whom I trust, both suggested that I share additional thoughts, about the climb, and about Hugh and losing him. In general, I don't share my emotions and feelings, and outside the brotherhood, often go to lengths to avoid even the perception of wild claims.

The truth of it is that at that time, I didn't know what to think, nor was I really thinking about it either. There was no time to dwell on the subject, no manner of becoming distracted in the moment. We were not yet out of an extreme environment and could easily succumb to any number of accidents, simply becoming another set of numbers on the mountain's death list.

There would be a few nightmares and sudden middle-of-the-night sobbing episodes a couple of months later, and I would miss Hugh's acerbic wit that out-matched Brian's and his sometimes wonderful comments. In base camp on a bright sunny day just after a cloudy, cold, windy one with blowing snow, my journal entry reads:

Fri 22 Feb. What a beautiful morning. Spirits soar. As Hugh says, "too bad you can't bottle the sun," and it perfectly encapsulated the thoughts of the three of us at that moment.

12

El Viento Blanco and the Wild Ride

In getting ready for the night, I took my boots off and finally looked at my feet. They were of some kind of dull color, not flesh-like at all, more like those of dead bodies I had recovered over the years and cold as ice to the touch. I didn't want to think about the full extent of the consequences. I needed to think on the here, now, and immediate future. I put my boots, crampons and exterior gloves and mitts in the vestibule of the tent. Our single remaining rope and all remaining climbing gear were outside the tent. We drifted off into a fitful sleep.

I was awakened by the sound of the tent flapping, shaking and vibrating with the wind. Then I became aware the wind was howling, roaring. I had no idea what the wind speed was, but it seemed greater, much greater, than what I experienced in a three-day, 50-60 mph storm at 18,000 feet on Denali. For several hours, the wind shrieked, and I could hear tent seams popping and an occasional ripping sound in the tent fabric.

I hoped against hope that the wind was transient, and not the beginning of a multi-day storm. I didn't think we could survive such a storm where we were and still make it off the mountain alive. Any high peak will have severe winds at times, often the result of uneven heating on mountain surfaces, and not necessarily an indication of a storm. On Aconcagua, high wind on or near the summit is often referred to as the Viento Blanco or White Wind. From below, you can usually see the indication of fierce winds by a lenticular shaped cloud that caps the summit or is hovering above it. Whether this was the true Viento Blanco and going to pummel us for days or not, I didn't know.

After a while, however, the wind subsided somewhat, and I could get some sleep.

I awoke suddenly in the morning, aware of Brian in his bag, on top of me. I was being forced onto the side of the tent on the downhill side of the platform. I thought I felt the edge of the tent platform underneath me give way very slightly, and I became quite concerned. "Brian, get off me," I said. Brian replied that he couldn't as there was too much snow on top of his side of the tent. He couldn't move. I was now getting desperate as I could definitely feel the tent shifting downhill.

"Brian, you *have* to get off – the tent platform is going to collapse!" I said.

"I'm trying," he replied.

Then in slow motion, the tent began to roll sideways off the tent platform, the anchors pulled out, and we began sliding down the upper reaches of the Canaleta and then straight down the fall line.

In March 1980, it was all snow in the upper reaches of the Canaleta. The tent was sliding and spinning on the snow slope, doing 360 degree turns with us inside, still in our sleeping bags. With every rotation, clothing, gear and equipment were being ejected through the rips and tears in the fabric. I knew from basic route study and the quick glance from the evening before that there were a couple of small cliffs and rock ledges along the sides of the Canaleta. If the tent (with us in it) were to slide too far, it would not be good. To this day, I don't know how or why the tent stopped and came to a rest, but it did. As I was thinking, *we need to cut this thing open and see what we have,* Brian takes a tiny penknife he carried on a necklace chain around his neck and does just that. I stick my head out first and see Brian's axe, still thrust through one of the anchor tie-down points. I was able to grab it and with a good swing, I got a solid purchase into the ice.

Detachedly, I realized we were in a slightly less steep part of the slope – sort of a small, tilted depression or bowl. I estimated everything around and above us to be between 30 to 40 degrees in angle, about the angle of a blue ski run just where your adrenaline kicks in.

I clipped the runner on the outside of the tent onto the axe and then clipped us into the runner on the inside....and I realized, *I'm using the damn thing after all.* Clipped in, the tent shouldn't go anywhere, and we should be okay. The tent had no shape and was draped around us; it was not possible to see if we were lying on its side or top. As we squirmed around inside the tent, with everything on the downhill side, we realized that if we were not careful, what remained was going to fall out through one of the tears, which was also on the downhill side. We took inventory and discovered that Brian's boots and gloves were nowhere to be seen. I had put my boots and gloves in the vestibule the evening before, which now of course was completely empty. Poking my head back out the hole Brian had cut and looking around outside the tent confirmed that we had equipment, gear and clothing scattered all the way up to the former tent site, just below the ridge.

What was going to be problematic was how to navigate from the shredded tent on a 30 to 40-degree snow and ice slope with no boots, no crampons, and no gloves and no axe. The one axe we had at that moment was the only thing holding the tent in place.

I volunteered to go and get everything as I figured what damage had been done to my feet was already done. I hoped that what more occurred would be minimal. So, I started up the slope in my borrowed inner boots with their smooth leather sole. I quickly found I had no purchase at all, and the snow was too hard to gently step into. I was going to have to kick steps or figure something out. I didn't relish the idea of attempting to kick steps with frozen feet in slippers – apart from being a bit painful, I assumed there was a real possibility of further injury if I did that. You could easily have kicked steps into it with a boot...but my boots were several hundred feet above me.

I found I could make adequate steps for my feet by punching and digging into the slope with my hands. Of course, I didn't have gloves, only fingerless mittens. So, I was probably looking at frostbite on my fingers too, but the only option I could see was not acceptable.

By making footsteps with my hands, then taking one foot at a time between my hands and gently placing it into the footstep just created, I was able to stand and take one step uphill. It was also the only way to tell if my foot was actually all the way into the step, since I couldn't feel my feet, much less how deep my foot was placed into the step. It was somewhat slow and laborious, but it was all I had.

Somewhere about halfway up I began thinking that what I was doing was not a good idea. It was wicked cold on my legs and hands. Apart from freezing more tissue, I didn't need to start trembling or shaking uncontrollably, or I would be worse off.

For the most part I remained focused and tried not to think about my exposure, literally and figuratively. While the Canaleta was not too steep and not technical, I was, after all, in the equivalent of smooth leather bottomed slippers, with frozen feet, on a snow and ice slope of 30 degrees with no axe and no way to arrest if I slipped and began sliding.

I was more than acutely aware of my situation. It was insane. I didn't want to consider the possibilities. They were all bad. But of all things, I was not going to simply wait and do nothing, or to rest until things got better. That would have been the surest way to arrive at the point where I couldn't do anything at all. Besides, I had told Brian I would go up and retrieve our stuff – so I would. I narrowed my focus again and concentrated on the space about four feet around me and nowhere else. I finally made it up to the previous night's tent site and the bulk of the gear.

I had found and picked up Brian's boots, and I could see mine, but they were over to the side a ways. I decided to put on his boots as mine might be too tight, and I didn't have the dexterity to put on my crampons – my fingers had lost all sensation. To use my boots, I would have to put the crampons on in order to hold the flapping sole onto the boot. Assessing the situation, I figured that I was probably not going to need crampons much longer but collected them anyway. I was forced into the realization of just how bad the sole on my right boot was, and the further problems of walking out were sinking in. The flap was completely detached along the welt for the first six inches of the boot. It took me a while longer, but I gathered everything I thought we'd need and descended to Brian. While descending slowly, I angled toward and passed by everything of ours that I could see and added one or two items to my load. I could not find our second camera – *was it still in the tent and I had somehow missed it?* Continuing down the slope, it took more than several minutes to reach the tent and Brian. He was sitting on the tent at this point and helped me get his boots off and he put them on quickly. Then he helped me get mine on along with my crampons. We took inventory, finished dressing, and repacked our rucksacks

Brian related this part of the climb later to me and friends and interviews as follows:

> *"...About 4 in the morning a storm started and by 7:30 it had completely destroyed our tent, and it collapsed from the weight of the snow onto me. I rolled over onto Mike - the weight was keeping me pinned to him - and the whole thing broke loose and we started down the ice hill. We went down about 300 feet."*

> *"The tent was ripped to shreds, our equipment was scattered all over the mountain... I had removed my boots while we were in the tent and had nothing on my feet. Mike, in a set of inner boots alone, was able to climb 300 feet above on the ice, in the equivalent of tennis shoes, with no ice axe, to get my boots from the ridge. Mike, who takes a size 9 boot, found my size 13 boots, put them on and strung a rope back to me. I had held on to the remainder of the tent with my bare hands to keep from losing the*

rest of our gear (through the rips and tears in the tent fabric). It was about 20 or 30 degrees below zero Fahrenheit. This whole ordeal started around 7:30 a.m. and was not finished until 2:30 p.m."

As Brian helped me with my boots and crampons, he was staring at the soles, and began to realize just how bad my boot situation was. We decided we had no option but to discard the ripped and shredded tent and a few other odds and ends and, feeling bad to leave more trash on the mountain, did so. We (at least I) were in, or rapidly approaching, a survival situation.

The one thing we were sorely missing was our second Leica SLR camera. It had not been in the tent after the slide and despite my best effort to find it on the climb to the ridge and descent back to Brian, I had not been able to do so. The other Leica, much of our film in general, and **all** our film from the face were with Hugh. I was now supremely grateful I had decided to take along my little Kodak Pocket Instamatic, as the photos from it would be the only ones of Brian and me on the summit.

13

Summit

Standing on the snow slope, amidst the remains of our shredded tent and other bits and pieces of our gear, thinking only of survival at this point, Brian said, "come on, let's go," and started to head downhill.

I told him, "No, we haven't summited yet – we haven't **stood** on the summit."

He looked at me, incredulous, and started to argue. He was basically saying that we had made it and we should just head down.

So close...At that point, we were still where the tent had stopped on its wild ride down the slope. We were about 200 vertical feet below the Guanaco Ridge (or Fila de Guanaco), just below the col, a little to the south and west of the Canaleta proper, which, looking uphill, lay to our left. We were about 500 vertical feet below the summit, and perhaps 400 yards away. It had taken me probably two hours just to climb back up to the tent site in my inner boots, bare hands and no axe. And there I was, telling Brian I wanted to climb it again, push on and not descend yet.

Persistent.

In our condition, we were looking at least two or three hours, perhaps more, all the way to the summit.

I was adamant and told him, "I am going to the summit. I'm doing it because I can, and for Hugh. I'm doing it so that when I tell someone I summited via the South Face, I can look at myself in the mirror afterwards."

March 14, 1980: South Summit and the Guanaco Ridge.

Brian was once again pissed at me, even though he knew I was right. I led back up the slope we had slid down inside the tent and that I was now climbing for the second time. As we slowly gained the Guanaco Ridge, turned left and headed toward the summit, I fell into a rhythm of short steps with two deep breaths between each step. Every ten steps or so I would take about five to ten breaths and repeat. I forced myself into my 'zone,' trying not to think about our situation. Even though all the food was gone, most of the stove fuel was gone along with the battered and shredded tent and some of the climbing gear, we were still carrying 30 or more pounds of gear. Progress was steady, but very slow. My frozen feet were painful somewhere in the recesses of my mind, and my hands were smarting pretty badly. During my climb to recover our gear and equipment after the sleigh ride in our tent, I thought my fingers had partially frozen while digging footsteps in the snow and ice barehanded. The fact that they were hurting, and I could feel the stinging pain was actually a good indication that perhaps all I had suffered was frost nip.

Once on the ridge proper, the longer rests every 10 steps or about once every 30 seconds, allowed me to begin looking around. The view was incredible. I was looking to the south, down and along the Face and it was spectacular, majestic, arcing between the two summits. The drop was so precipitous on the south side. Any sane person would not want to get too close. Even though we had climbed it and been in its vertical world for two weeks, in the space of just a few hours, we were now back to having the ground actually underneath us, with our feet upon it.

After a little more progress, we reached the small summit plateau and were weaving all over, looking at this and at that, as if drunk. If there had been an observer, they would have thought we were crazy. But we were alone on the mountain, there was no one else on the summit, there were no tents anywhere down below, no one on any of the trails, no movement of any kind that we could see. We had not seen a soul for almost a month.

We found the box for the summit register, but with no register. The only thing we had that we could leave as a token was an Argentinian coin. We dedicated the coin to Hugh and placed it in the box.

Brian began to lead out for the descent, and I stopped him, again. He had that '*now* what?' look. I reached into the inner pocket of my parka and pulled out my Kodak Pocket Instamatic camera – the one that I had told him and Hugh would be with me on the summit if everything else went to hell. He was momentarily speechless and then grinned hugely. We took a few pictures of us on the summit and of the summit plateau with the Face in the background.

In spite of everything, at that moment I felt strangely, weirdly, content. *Now*, I thought, *we can descend.*

The author on the summit, with the rope indicating the climbers' crazy path (photo by Brian Berg).

March 14, 1980: Brian on the summit.

March 14, 1980: The author on the summit (photo by Brian Berg).

14

Descent

Brian led out and down toward the Canaleta and I stumbled behind him trying to keep up. My borrowed boots were now causing me to nearly trip with every other step. Even with my crampons on, snow had bunched up between the layers of the sole, adding to my clumsiness due to not being able to feel much of anything below my ankle. I was going to have to cut off the part of the Vibram sole that was flapping. We managed to find a sheltering rock known as La Cueva (The Cave). There, we spent the night. We had no water again and had no food at all for three days, but we were blessed to be in a shelter of sorts. I worked on my boots, cutting away the flapping sole. I could barely work the knife and found I had no fine dexterity with my fingers. While I was now rid of the flap of Vibram sole that was catching on everything, I had exposed an ultra-slick plastic plate that was part of the mid-sole. The boot from the heel forward was now like a mini ski, no treads, no friction and very slippery.

The next morning, we continued down the slope toward a hut we could see far below in the distance. We took a bit of time in scanning below from side to side but could still see no sign of anyone on the mountain. There was still no movement, no bright colors of any tents or parkas. We did see one of the main climbing routes from the north side which was a well-defined trail that veered off to our right as we looked downslope. Well below us, it eventually looped back around to the hut. We were not having any part of any extra distance whatsoever. We started to descend in a direct line. The going was treacherous and very slow. Much of the exposed rock was loose.

The first time my feet slid out from under me and I landed on my butt I realized I needed to plan every step. Every part of every step. I needed to consciously think about where, exactly, to step, which way to place my feet and how to angle the boot. And most importantly, with each step, which way to twist my body in case I fell in order to land on my pack or my ass and not do a header or break some part of me not already injured. It was slow. As my toes and feet thawed, the pain increased. My feet felt like they were continuing to swell, and I became concerned that when my boots were finally removed, they wouldn't be able to go back on. If that happened before I reached civilization, I would be truly screwed. At some point on the descent, my fingertips started turning black and I had very little fine muscle movement in my hands. I don't think Brian realized just how much difficulty I was having. He finally got some idea of my condition when I asked him to unzip my pants as I needed to pee, and I couldn't get my fly open. I told him I could handle the rest...

My urine was dark – a deep brownish yellow. I was surprised I could pee at all given our state of dehydration. My clothes were hanging on my frame. (Six days later, when I checked into the hospital in Portland and eating every chance I could along the way, I weighed 127 pounds, down from my then normal weight of 155-160. I had lost over 30 pounds from the ordeal in two and half weeks.)

Some medical texts and people say that frostbitten tissue doesn't hurt as it is numb – frozen. I can tell you that the interface between frozen and viable tissue can hurt quite a bit, and even more as the frozen parts thaw. In the case of frostbitten feet or toes, the recommended and classic way to prevent any additional, post-injury damage, is to avoid walking and to be carried down the mountain. Unfortunately, we could not see a soul anywhere – no climbers, no tents and no movement. And I wasn't going to wait. Progress though, was very slow.

One of the mind games I was doing at this point was composing letters in my head to the senior members of my PJ team in Portland. I remember singling out Mike Cooney, George Selfridge, Phil Brady and Dave Ward. Each letter was personalized, with specific comments about what I respected in each of them, how we had interacted, and what I hoped for upon return. Of course, the letters were never written, except in my head, but I found it somehow important to let each one know what I was thinking.

We reached the hut in the late afternoon and had already decided we were going to spend the night. Brian had arrived ahead of me and had good news. He had found food inside and there was a tiny bit of water available as well. It seemed like a feast.

The next morning, we started out down the well-trodden trail following the drainage of the Horcones Superior Glacier. Brian was immediately ranging way in front. We didn't speak, but even without talking I knew he was going on ahead and would send help or rescue back when he got to civilization. I continued on as I could. I was absolutely, categorically, not going to sit down and wait. In a very short time, I lost track of Brian.

The trail was undulating, sometimes near the river, sometimes well above to the side. Wherever there was any incline in the trail, each part of every step was thought out, planned, slow and deliberate. As I continued, I found myself needing to cross the river and had somehow missed where the trail did so. At first, I couldn't figure out how to descend to the river without needing to down climb steep broken rock. I wasn't up to that. I stumbled on a little farther.

Eventually I found myself at the river's edge. Small gain, however, it was very rocky, and the river had lots of small rapids. Here, the flowing water was more of a mountain stream really, threading its way through rock debris and the remnants of snowpack ice. I didn't want to have to cross this thing more than once. Scanning the other side of the river, I could see the trail both up- and down-valley from where I was, so I knew I should cross here if possible. The sides of the river were about 25 to 50 yards apart at this point and downstream from me the valley side I was on was pretty steep with no trail. I figured out I was not going to be able to continue further down valley without crossing.

Trying to visualize a crossing and plan my steps, I finally decided on a spot with several flat rocks part way across, and then a shallow looking area of calm water about 10-15 feet wide adjacent to the one- to two-foot-high embankment on the other side of the river. I decided to go for it and, just before stepping off the flat rocks, remembered to unbuckle the waist band of my pack. If left buckled and the water was deep – over my head deep – because the pack would initially float, it would instantly put me face down in the water, pulling my feet off the bottom.

The first and second steps through the water were fine, perhaps knee-deep but on submerged wide, stable rocks. Then there was another "fuck" moment. On the next step I was in water over my head. I was fighting to keep my head up and from being swept toward faster moving water. I was now quite concerned – pretty freaked out, I guess you could say. Adrenaline flashed and I was able to dog paddle and bob, pushing off the bottom toward the other side. My pack was indeed floating, but with the waist band disconnected, it was not forcing me onto my stomach. The embankment that would have been easy to climb was now a couple of feet over my head and I was looking ahead at a vertical mud wall.

I mentally recalled a scene from a few years before when I had been assisting the Riverside Mountain Rescue Unit (an outstanding group of folks) as an extra body on a search of a desert canyon for a missing hiker. I was assigned to help with sweeping the side of a probable line of descent for signs of a forced path or trail and I heard one of the senior members of the RMRU say something to the effect that he thought they'd find the person in a pool in the middle of the canyon. Other hikers had been found in the same manner. I thought to myself there was no way I was going to be found in a pool in a mountain stream after everything I had been through.

Grunting and screaming, I punched my hands into the mud trying to find or make purchase. Grasping anything I could, I scrambled up onto the top of the embankment, collapsed and was scared. I was drenched, cold and shaking. Slowly, I calmed down, and taking stock of the situation, I realized my clothing was designed to function and keep me warm when wet, I still had my pack, minimal equipment and my sleeping bag. I figured one way to dry off was to move on.

So I did. I filled up my water bottles, gained the trail and continued shuffling, plodding on. I think I stayed mostly on the trail, though at times it switched back and I lost it, and then gained it again. It got dark, very dark. There was no moon at all – it was 16 days into the lunar cycle from the full moon the day before we started. My headlamp was useless; its batteries had died days before. I continued anyway as I could feel the difference in my feet and legs between being on the trail and off. This was a trick I had developed when traveling at night in the field during my early days as a PJ. It's an old skill really – thousands of years old – and anyone who must walk at night through a forest, across remote terrain or off road will develop it. Today of course, it's easier to use night vision equipment.

After a while it sunk in that maybe my pain and damaged feet were not helping with the "feeling the trail thing." I had to admit that I had well and truly lost the trail, and the river was far below me. I stopped, deciding not to take another step, and at my feet found a small hollow, an almost level spot in the rocks. And there I crashed for the night. I was able to get my sleeping bag and pad out and actually got some rest. The next morning as I sat up and looked around, I saw that not more than three feet in front of me, in the direction I had been going, was a 300-foot vertical drop off. I had no idea then – or now – why I stopped at that exact moment. The bitch of it was, however, that I needed to turn around, backtrack and descend 300 feet back down to the river's edge.

While I was packing up my few things, I could plainly hear gunshots and realized a rescue party was somewhere in the valley. The gunshots were repeated a few minutes later and I determined they were below my position and down valley. After a minute or so of scanning, I was able to locate movement of what appeared to be uniformed people on horses. They didn't see or hear me and slowly proceeded down the valley out of sight.

I made it down to the trail and kept on shuffling, soon finding myself at Confluencia. Our cache was still there, but I was just not up to recovering it. But it was another water stop, however. In a trance, hardly aware if I was conscious, I kept going, not sure when or if I would see someone. At that point though, I knew I could make the highway – maybe not that same day, but eventually. Hours later, by then late afternoon, I looked up and saw the men on horseback again, appearing as if from a dream, staring at me, and for a fleeting moment I considered joking about how I was okay and didn't really need a lift or a ride.

Fortunately, reality set in and one soldier took my pack while two others helped me onto a horse behind one of the men. They looked at me as if I was from another planet, not sure what to make of this emaciated, sunburned "Norte Americano" who had summited with frozen feet, descended the mountain to Plaza de Mulas, and then walked over 20 miles to where we were now.

When we reached Cruz de Caña and the lodge, I ended up in an ambulance and the first stop was the military outpost I remembered from the visit for our permit. I felt like a zombie or freak as everyone was staring. Confusion reigned when I asked about Brian. It was clear he was not here at that moment, but I didn't understand what they were telling me. They explained they would take me to the hospital in Mendoza where I would receive treatment.

I was placed in a different ambulance, with no windows of course, so I couldn't see where we were going. After an hour or so, we stopped and the doors were thrown open, and Brian was there. Our reunion was emotional, as neither of us was sure until that point that the other was still alive.

Brian later filled me in on what had transpired with him. He told me he had made the road to Mendoza about 11 p.m. and was run-walking toward Puente del Inca. An ambulance appeared, picked him up and took him to the military post where his hands and feet were treated for frostbite. He said they sent a truck that night to begin a search for me to no avail.

He had spent the night there and in the morning was able to convince the military to send out people on horseback to search farther up the valley. He recounted to the authorities how Hugh had died and shortly after that he had been arrested by the Argentinian police. Brian said they confiscated his money and passport and took him to the nearest city. There they questioned him in Spanish, which he didn't understand. He said all he knew was that I was alone on the mountain, he didn't know exactly where, that Hugh was dead and that he (Brian) was in the middle of nowhere with no money and no passport.

On to the hospital in Mendoza.

Brian and I were placed in different bays, or large rooms, each with about 10 beds, well-spaced apart. Most of my toes were now turning black and the distal part of each foot was waxy, bluish-white looking. That I had severe frostbite was beyond doubt at this point – mentally, I went back to the question I posed to myself during the bivy at 22,000 feet: *How much?*

I spent a fitful night.

In the morning there was a flurry of activity and excitement in the room – in everybody present as well. A television crew and reporters had arrived and were setting up at the hospital. We were to be on Argentinian national news.

In a remarkable coincidence, the doctor who had first seen Brian in the village was the son of the head of the province's mountaineering association. Brian had told him of the climb and the doctor had told his father. That afternoon and overnight, they had mobilized members of the climbing community, confirmed our ascent, got the police to release Brian, recovered Brian's passport and our money, and picked up our bags from storage at the hotel. He also coordinated for the Argentinian military to recover our cache from Confluencia and arranged for our flight back to the U.S.

And, he had spoken to the press.

There, in front of the cameras – I wasn't sure I understood more than two words of what was being said, but we smiled and nodded a lot and were embarrassed by our 15 minutes of fame.

Interview over, Brian explained that our flight back home was leaving in about 45 minutes and that we needed to hustle and to step lively. I didn't quite laugh. We now had several people helping us, however, and I found myself bodily picked up and set down into a wheelchair.

At the airport, they were holding the airplane for us and I was carried up the boarding stairs and plopped down into a seat at the very front that had extra legroom. Homeward bound, we had a few hours delay in Santiago, Chile, and ended up downtown at one of the many superb seafood market restaurants. We were ravenous.

Continuing on to the U.S., I was a little concerned about being pulled from the flight as I was incapable of much self-assistance, but Brian was there to run interference (and undo my zipper as required). We were met at the airport in El Paso by friends and Brian's wife, and then back to Holloman AFB.

The reunion with friends and Brian's family was a BBQ affair and was both something wonderful and something painful. I couldn't cut anything, could barely grasp a piece of chicken or a rib with my fingers, but it was soooo good.

I was totally amazed and very grateful that Jeff Murphy, one of my PJ buddies from the 303rd ARRSq, and his family were there as well. I don't how they worked that out, but it was great to see them. The next morning Brian checked into the hospital on base and since I was with him, they checked me in as well. The doctors and staff began looking at treatment options and realized that I needed to get back to Portland. With more help from friends, I got my flight arranged, found myself back at the airport in El Paso and finally arrived in Portland six days after making the summit.

In the American Alpine Journal publication of 1981, Volume 23, Issue 55, page 237, Brian tersely summarizes our climb as follows:

> *Aconcagua, South Face, Messner Route. Mike French, Englishman Hugh Grandfield and I set our Base Camp at the Plaza Francia on February 19. After ten days of acclimatizing, we started up the route, hoping to make the second ascent of it and the first alpine ascent. Unseasonably heavy snowfall and unusually bad weather caused major*

delays. On March 13 at 22,300 feet in a change of lead, Grandfield sustained a fatal fall when for some reason he completely unhooked his rope to effect the change-over. Unable to reach the summit that day, French and I bivouacked on the Guanaco Ridge. The cold and wind were fierce and French and I were both frostbitten in the ensuing storm. We reached the summit on March 14.

Brian A. Berg, USAF Pararescue Team

Epilogue

Over the next six months I had four operations. The first was to amputate nine and three-quarter toes. The others were to provide primary closure on the ends of my feet. The wounds on my right leg healed without a problem and the scars blended in with others. I suffered very minor tissue loss on the tips of the fingers on my right hand, and to my pleasant surprise, have experienced no hyper-sensitivity to cold on either hand since.

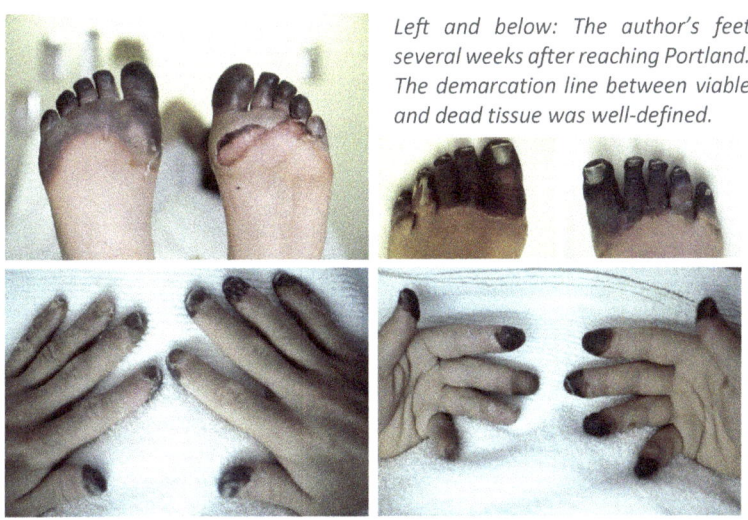

Left and below: The author's feet several weeks after reaching Portland. The demarcation line between viable and dead tissue was well-defined.

Above: The author's frostbitten hands. At the time of the photos, it was still too early to tell if there was permanent damage.

I had one fixed goal at the time: I wanted to continue as an operational PJ. That was awkward, but I had help. I ended up becoming first non-current, then un-qualified as I couldn't do much of anything in the hospital. Once leaving the hospital, I still didn't have decent skin closure on the stumps of my feet, so could not run or do very much physical activity. However, as the NCOIC of the section, a large part of my job was admin related, and that was something I could do. My squadron CO and OPs officers at the time basically fended off an admin re-assignment to another job, pending rehabilitation, a medical evaluation and re-qualification. I remain grateful to Lt. Col. Mike Peters, Maj. Pinar Crane and Capt. John Baczuk.

With time, I was able to rehabilitate, began working out and training on the side to do the tasks and skills I used to do with ease. Because I had also been medically disqualified from being a PJ, I would need a medical waiver – though nobody I could reach out to knew of one being given for my injuries in recent history. Then, if granted the waiver, I would need to requalify. Once I was sure I could pass the Pararescue physical fitness test and any skill test they could throw at me, I sought out our supporting medical unit. With the recommendation of a friendly and progressive thinking flight surgeon, I submitted a request to the Air Force and received what at the time was a rare "functional" waiver for the loss of digits from my feet. That allowed me to regain flying, jump and dive status.

Once I regained status, I was very focused on the re-qual and I had fantastic support from the majority of the team and the squadron in general. My final re-qual exercise and evaluation included an ingress to a recovery area on an island with a night river swim and hike, recovery of an item, then an exfil with another night swim back to shore. My main teammate during this evaluation was Bob Bergstrom, with whom I reconnected in 2018 and more recently in 2021. He was then one of my newbies and is now one of my sailing mentors.

Afterward

I retired from the Air Force in the early 1990s and began a second career working as a Special Agent for the U.S. Department of State, Bureau of Diplomatic Security. Like everyone in the Foreign Service, I traveled some, and outside of near constant TDYs (or deployments), I was assigned to Washington D.C.; Lima, Peru; Los Angeles, Havana, Cuba; Tunis, Tunisia and Bogotá, Colombia. In 2005, I retired from the Department of State in Bogotá while assigned to the U.S. Embassy.

I returned to the U.S. in 2009.

Today, my passion is sailing, and my latest project was a 7,250-mile voyage from Oceanside, California, to Hawaii and back. It included a 2,800-mile solo sail from Hawaii to the U.S. Pacific Northwest. And, after cruising in that area for a month, I returned south along the West Coast back to my home marina in Oceanside.

Glossary

AFB   Air Force Base

Alpine Style   Carrying all food and equipment
                   as one climbs, not relying on
                   porters, with no fixed lines and
                   no intermediate camps to stage
                   from and return to before moving
                   to a higher spot on the mountain.

APU   Auxiliary Power Unit

ARRS   Aerospace Rescue and Recovery
                   Service

ARRSq   Aerospace Rescue and Recovery
                   Squadron

Bergschrund   A crevasse that forms at the head
                   of a glacier, where the moving ice
                   of the glacier separates from the
                   headwall or ice on the rock

above. It often extends down to bedrock so can be quite deep. A bergschrund is often filled in with snow early in the climbing season, offering an easy (but careful) transition from the glacier to the ice or headwall above it. It can be a major obstacle in an otherwise accessible route or line on the mountain.

Bivy   Short for bivouac. Technically, a temporary camp without tent or cover, used especially by soldiers or mountaineers. Here I also use it occasionally to denote an improvised, less-than-adequate tent site.

Fast Rope   A technique of deploying from a hovering helicopter to the surface by sliding down a thick rope. Can be done to the ground, water, or a vessel in the water.

FNG   Fucking New Guy

Free Fall Swimmer Deployment	A technique of deploying from a helicopter overwater, generally while the helicopter is in forward flight at 10 knots and 10 feet.
Moraine	A mass of rocks and sediment carried down and deposited by a glacier, typically as ridges at its edges or extremity
NCOIC	Non-Commissioned Officer in Charge
Pin	Short for piton. A metal spike driven into a crack or crevice in rock by a hammer which can be used as a point of protection or suspension.
PJ	Pararescueman. Sometimes referred to (erroneously) as Parachute Jumper
Recce	Short for reconnaissance. I use it as both a noun and a verb.

Serac

A block or vertical column of a broken section of ice. Usually at the intersection of crevasse lines and at the downhill edge or terminus of a glacier. They can be house sized or much larger. They are the part of the glacier most likely to fall or move suddenly – hence a danger to a climber below.

SERE

Survival, Evasion, Resistance, Escape. Both an area of training and expertise and now a specialty in the Air Force and other U.S. forces.

Stem

A climbing technique in which the hands and/or feet are pressured in opposition far out to each side, as in a dihedral or wide chimney. Picture a door frame or narrow corridor and putting your feet and hands on opposite sides and using counter-pressure to hold in place and move upward like a worm.

TDY

Temporary Duty. Today often referred to by the military as a deployment. An assignment of temporary nature to a particular place, unit, or base that is not one's home station.

About the Author

 Michael French is an adventurer and a calculated risk-taker with a live-life-to-its fullest attitude and roll-with-the punches spirit. After a distinguished military career and retirement from the United States Air Force, Mike served in the State Department as a foreign service officer. The combination of experiences that colored his younger years in the military, the events of his second career, and the fortitude gained from his adrenaline-pumping hobbies have made him into who he is today. Now spending much of his time on the water, and with the energy of a teenager, Mike maintains and sails his beloved Ericson sailboat on the waters of Southern California and beyond, days, weeks and sometimes months at a time. When not at sea or at the marina, Mike resides in the coastal town of Encinitas with his wife, Patty, who indulges Mike's desire to explore and push limits, understanding and accepting that Mike hasn't yet "got it out of his system."

www.ingramcontent.com/pod-product-compliance
Lightning Source LLC
Chambersburg PA
CBHW051619120626
46551CB00014B/1869